It's Showtime!

Butterfield Speaks on The Power of Persuasion

Communication and Presentation Skills
for Business and Legal Professionals

by Richard Butterfield

edited by Steven Young

STEVE - BETH

Love Love love

San Francisco, California
2008

ISBN-13: 978-0-615-15785-6

Library of Congress Control Number: 2008901161

It's Showtime!

Butterfield Speaks on
The Power of Persuasion

Communication and Presentation Skills
for Business and Legal Professionals

Dedication

For my father

As a boy growing up in Hingham, Massachusetts, I romanticized my father's life. He ran a CBS television station that was sorely in need of a turn-around man when he arrived. Hero that he was, he pushed the station's local newscast to #1 in the market. He had already done the same thing at a station in Minneapolis and he would go on to do it again in Portland, Oregon. But in Hingham, I actually imagined workers at the station cheering for him. In fact, I still have a 5th grade writing assignment in which I described all those passionate employees chanting "RJB! RJB! Who's the greatest? RJB!"

As I grew older, I looked back with some embarrassment on my youthful fantasies of my father's work life. Who in their right mind would cheer a business executive? But today, I coach people like my father. And I've learned that, while people may not actually stand up and cheer, they do something much more powerful – they engage, they join, they find purpose and bet their futures on persuasive leaders like my dad.

Here's to you, RJB – you were the greatest.

Contents

Introduction:
The Passion to Persuade

We've all seen them, heard them, experienced their power. In business, education, the arts and media and, of course, politics. They are the CEOs who emerge from the executive ranks. The gurus who guide the experts. The true teachers who stand out among the educators. The statesmen and women who rise above mere politicians and officeholders.

What they say, and how they say it, has the power of persuasion. With that power, they command not just attention but allegiance. They inspire. By giving voice to their vision, they convince us that we see it, too. Like Prometheus, they bring us a gift of fire, kindling their passion in our hearts and minds. Through the power of persuasion, they make things happen. They move and they shake. They change the world – or at least they change minds, which is the same thing.

How can we understand their peculiar genius? Are they "naturals" – prodigious talents sprung full-blown from the gene pool? Do they have more brainpower or willpower, exceptional competitive drive, or the ineffable quality we call charisma?

Maybe they're simply more glib than the rest of us, blessed with the gift of gab and nerves of steel. Maybe they're better at thinking and talking "on their feet," as the expression goes. Or maybe they're just plain lucky – fortunate enough to be linked by history to a welcome message, a winning product, a prosperous enterprise, or a great cause.

After all, few people in history have had or ever will have the oratorical power of Lincoln or Churchill or Martin Luther King, Jr, much less an opportunity to use that power to save a nation or advance a great cause. Only a handful are both forceful and fortunate enough to imprint their passion on public perception and drive revolutions in business and technology, as Jack Welch, Steve Jobs, and John Chambers have done.

But look closer to home. Most of us have known exceptional communicators in our own lives and careers – friends and colleagues, mentors and managers with a talent and zest for touching others through the spoken word.

Look near as well as far, and you'll find that the passion to persuade is alive and at work every day, in everyone's life, including yours.

All the World's a Stage

I devoted much of my education to becoming an actor, and I started my career as a theater person. I "pounded the boards" in college productions at Stanford. I earned my master's degree in acting at the American Conservatory Theater in San Francisco, and later became Dean of the Conservatory. Meanwhile, I enjoyed several years of success as an actor, director, and teacher of theater arts in the Bay Area (and yes, a little bit in Hollywood).

During those years it never occurred to me that the craft I was practicing might be valuable, or even useful, for more than performing Shakespeare and Sondheim.

But, like most people, I kept up with the careers of friends and acquaintances in business, law, medicine, engineering, and other fields. All of these people were smart and capable. Many were truly exceptional. Yet, while some excelled and advanced as I expected they would, others seemed slow to fulfill their potential. It started me wondering about the latter group: did they lack some ingredient, some gift or skill, for success?

Then one day a trio of lawyers walked into my office at the American Conservatory Theater and asked me a simple question: "Can you help lawyers succeed, in the courtroom and beyond, by teaching them the skills used in theater?" My answer was "Yes," and my journey had begun.

My transition from actor, teacher, and director to communications consultant was inspired by the realization that the arts of the theater could be enormously useful to virtually everyone with drive and determination, whatever their field or profession.

The intense pursuit of an objective. The importance of clarity and focus. The impact of brevity. The art of storytelling. The meaning and power of body language. The effective use of the voice. And the value of preparation, practice, and rehearsal.

These are the elements that make up the power of persuasion. And they have just as much to do with presenting yourself effectively as they do with an actor's portrayal of Lady Macbeth, Willy Loman, Eliza Doolittle, or Cyrano de Bergerac. They come into play in a board meeting, a product launch, a press briefing, a client conference, a trial or negotiation, and hundreds of other presentations and interactions in business and professional life.

In short, these skills and techniques work as powerfully in the workaday world and everyday life as they do in the make-believe realm of the theater. They can and do help people succeed at work, in their careers, even in their personal lives. And they are available to all of us.

The Many Uses of Persuasion

It's Showtime: Butterfield Speaks on the Power of Persuasion is a guide for people who want to learn, develop, and master the art of persuasive communication through the spoken word.

The approach described here, which I call the power of persuasion for short, has been developed and refined during hundreds of workshops, coaching sessions, media trainings, and rehearsals. It has helped people in business, technology, health-care, law, advertising, and other professions. It will prepare you to succeed in press events, client conferences, roadshows, tradeshows, speeches, and business pitches.

Beyond preparing for specific events, you can count on the skills and techniques developed through the power of persuasion to help bring discipline and alignment to your company's branding, product positioning, and public relations. By crafting compelling messages and delivering them effectively in both normal and challenging circumstances – not only in one-to-many presentations and encounters, but also in one-on-one relationships – you'll be able to win agreement and change minds in your organization, your industry, the marketplace, and the forum of public opinion.

The power of persuasion is not about leadership as such, although I've coached many leaders and participated in many executive development programs. This is no accident. After all, communication is the action of leadership. It's the means that leaders use to translate their intellectual brilliance or political instincts or market insight or decision-making acumen into action. It's the way they project their will in the world, persuading others to believe, to join, to act. But those are challenges for all of us, not for leaders only. And so is the power of persuasion.

How This Book Is Organized

This book is divided into three major sections.

Part I, "Accessing the Power of Persuasion Within," covers the personal preparation necessary before you can either craft an effective message or communicate it successfully –

- getting in touch with your professional passion and making sure you have the right attitude
- developing the listening skills you need to know and connect with your audience and get across "what's in it for them"
- clarifying your vision so you can share it with others

Part II, "Discovering and Developing Your Message," is a guide to creating clear, compelling messages –

- risks and opportunities: assessing the event or occasion, your objectives, and what's at stake

- identifying the core of your message, or your "message mantra"
- "powerbites," storytelling, and other techniques for making your message memorable
- structuring a presentation

Part III, "Mastering Your Craft as a Communicator," provides tips and techniques for developing your tools as a speaker –

- the power of the voice
- taking control: acting as producer, director, and designer of your "show"
- body language: relaxing onstage, finding positions that work for you, and the power of gesture
- how to rehearse
- preparing for and handling Q&A sessions effectively

Three appendices provide tips for dealing with pre-presentation nerves; a checklist for evaluating presentations, your own and others'; and techniques for handling challenging situations primarily in interactive group workshops and training sessions.

At the end of certain chapters you'll find exercises for practicing and developing various communication skills. I urge you to use them on your own or with a colleague or friend to prepare, practice, and develop your power of persuasion.

Preparation, practice, development – these are three excellent notes on which to end this introduction, because mastering the power of persuasion is not a mystery. It's a matter of discovering and developing the passion to persuade, and the skills and techniques for doing so, that we all have within us.

Part I:
Accessing the Power of Persuasion

Chapter 1
Three Truths About Attitude

It may be true that most great speakers are born, not made. But consider the story of Demosthenes. As a youth in Athens, he had a speech impediment, and he was jeered the first time he addressed a large public assembly. So, to learn to speak distinctly, Demosthenes practiced talking with pebbles in his mouth and recited poetry while running. To strengthen his voice, he went to the seashore and declaimed over the roar of the waves. And to learn to craft compelling messages, he worked as a speechwriter for many years. Demosthenes made himself into an orator – the greatest, we are told, in ancient Greece.

Like Demosthenes, anyone can become a good speaker, maybe even a great one. And even good speakers can deliver great speeches by harnessing the power of persuasion.

Effective speeches and presentations come from careful preparation and rehearsal; much of this book is devoted to those tasks. But for most people, be-coming persuasive begins with some personal preparation. That's what this chapter is about.

The First Truth: *You are on a mission.*
Whatever their business or profession, the most successful leaders I've encountered all have one thing in common: they are on a mission. They are driven by an energy that emanates from the very core of their being. Four examples:

> J Allard, known for his work on both the Xbox and Zune music player at Microsoft, has a reputation inside and outside the com-pany as a visionary. Ask him about digital entertainment and you understand why. You're quickly swept up in J's inspiring vision of all the "What if?" and "Why not?" possibilities for the future of

digital devices and their place in our lives. You share his vision because you want to, and you can't wait to see it become a reality.

Dr. Robert Pearl is CEO of Northern California's Permanente Medical group, which includes thousands of Kaiser Permanente doctors. In all his communications, Dr. Pearl combines a surgeon's keen focus with an exuberant intellectual energy. When he talks to physicians about what they can do to improve patient care, he combines his encyclopedic knowledge with the sheer intensity of his belief to create an inspiring, contagious vision of a better, more effective way of practicing medicine.

Melanie Poturica, managing partner at the labor and employment law firm Liebert Cassidy Whitmore, radiates her sense of mission both in her listening and in her speaking. Just from the way she engages as a listener – empathetic and affirming all at once – Melanie's clients know how much she cares about them and their cause. And, while she's highly skilled in the bold and theatrical tactics of the courtroom, she also understands and uses the persuasive power of quiet intensity in a variety of circumstances.

"I was on a bike ride. Had an idea." That's how Gary Erickson describes the epiphany that led to his founding Clif Bar, the natural foods maker that became one of the fastest-growing companies in America. But with Gary, you don't hear standard CEO-talk about innovation or first-mover advantage. You hear about good nutrition, about wholesome products, about sustaining employees and communities and the planet. You understand why Gary rejected a nine-figure buy-out and kept control of his company. And you're glad he did, because you feel like he did it for you.

Leaders like these have a connection with their mission that is visceral in the original sense of that word: they feel it in their gut. And when we listen to them, we feel it, too. Passion is contagious. When we sense it in a speaker, we share it; the speaker's mission becomes our mission. That's why tapping into what really moves you is so important to developing your power of persuasion.

Call it your mission, your passion, your motivation: when connecting with it comes naturally to you, great. But when it doesn't, what then?

Then you have to work at it. You have to work at identifying what's important to you. You have to define your mission. You have to uncover your passion. It may lie deep inside you, and need to be hauled up into the light of day before you can articulate it. Or it may be "hiding in plain sight." It may even be visible to everyone but you. To connect with it, you may have to step back and take a fresh look at your experience or your daily activities, the choices you've made over time or the ones you make every day.

Take the time to talk through your mission, and I do mean talk. It's important to connect with what's at stake – and why it matters to you – not just in your thoughts or in writing, but with your speaking voice. The exercise at the end of this chapter provides a structured method for doing so. But there are many ways to go about this essential task.

As a start, you might want to read out loud the text of your organization's mission statement; if nothing else, it will serve as a baseline for defining what's at stake. But when you're onstage under the lights or alone at the podium, facing a board of directors or a gaggle of reporters, you will succeed only if you can draw on something much more personal. Chances are, you'll have to delve more deeply than a mission statement to uncover that.

You may want to think back to memorable moments in your life or career. Take time to remember – or talk to – a mentor or colleague who has played an important role in your professional development. Rereading a favorite poem, essay, or speech, or listening to a piece of music you've always loved, can also help open pathways to what really matters to you.

Don't back off from strong feelings. Everyone has a dream; don't be afraid of embracing yours. Envision what you want to achieve, what you want to be, what you want the world to be – that's what visionaries do. Then talk about it to a friend, colleague, spouse, or partner.

A couple of examples, starting with my own: As an actor, I often experienced those magical moments when great drama, well performed, moves an audience of hundreds of people to hold their breath in suspense, gasp with horror, or laugh with relief as if they were one person. I also loved to teach – for years, I had the privilege of passing on my knowledge in scene study, voice, and musical theater classes and watching young artists grow into their own talents. When I brought those two parts of my training and experience together, and started teaching business and professional people how to master the art of communication, I found a new sense of purpose that energizes and enriches my life to this day. It is just enormously satisfying to me – and incredibly fun – to help smart, committed people experience their own power of persuasion.

Here's an example of someone who had to do some digging to uncover her passion. This executive had been given responsibility for emergency preparedness at the many facilities of a large regional healthcare provider. It was a big job, and one that would require her to win the cooperation and orchestrate the efforts of many people. In my early training sessions with her, she came off as a dull, uninspired, and uninspiring speaker. She didn't communicate any sense of mission; listening to her, it was hard to feel that there was anything much at stake.

So we did some exploring. How had she come into her new job? Why did she care about what she was doing? What drew her to this career? Talking about such things brought her around to some disaster relief work she did years ago. As she recalled the devastation and loss, the shock and grief of those who suffered, she became emotional. Through this courageous exploration, her mission came into focus, and the stakes were very high indeed: by preparing people for emergencies, she wanted to avert the suffering that occurs when disaster strikes. Most important, she found a way to infuse this passion into her communications. Often starting her presentations with a story about why everyone needs to prepare for the unexpected, she captivates the audience with her energetic style and the sparkle in her eyes.

Discovering what drives you doesn't have to be like therapy. Simple but powerful ideas often emerge from the exercise "Uncovering Your Passion" at the end of this chapter. I've had clients "discover" themselves as problem solvers, change drivers, conductors, teachers, and corporate archeologists. And by connecting with their mission, by invoking it either directly or indirectly in their presentations, all of them have become more compelling and more persuasive.

Connecting with your passion isn't always a solo act. When presenting in groups, people often have to make an effort to get in touch with their mission both as individuals and as a group. For example, I once worked with a group of technology executives on the launch of an important new product. Five people were to have a role in the presentation, and even more had a chance to give their input as we developed the story they were going to tell.

As can often happen, in our drive to lock down the messaging – features and benefits, what's new and different, market position – we had sucked the life right out of the show. Before we could take the presentation to the audience, we had to regroup and ask each presenter the fundamental questions: Why do you care? Why are you so jazzed about this product? What's your personal stake in what you're saying? Each of the executives reconnected with the excitement he felt about the product and the process of developing it – the challenge of solving problems in innovative ways, the thrill of competition, the inevitability of progress, the sheer fun of creating something new. And before long, each of them had figured out how to weave his passion into his presentation.

These executives did what I call a gut-check. When athletes and soldiers use that expression, they're talking about summoning the grit it takes to fight through adversity, to overcome obstacles, to win. In relation to the power of persuasion, it's about making sure that you are on a mission, that your passion is fully engaged in what you have to say. In short, do you feel it in your gut?

Whether as an individual or as a team, you'll always connect better with your audience by connecting with what really moves you. When you project your own excitement, the people you're addressing can't help but feel it themselves. Whether you're convincing a jury, selling a product, driving a culture change, or sharing a vision, your passion is your most powerful ally.

The Second Truth: *It's your job.*

Unless you're in marketing or public relations, you might not think of yourself as being engaged in a communications campaign as part of your professional responsibilities.

But you are, every day – or at least every day you're at work.

In this age of e-mail, voicemail, and instant messaging, it's easy to forget that face-to-face communication is an important part of every job. One-on-one or one-to-many, you make presentations all the time. It's how you get things done.

In a word, it's your job.

And if it's your job to communicate, then it's your responsibility to communicate with all the power at your command. As long as you collect those paychecks, you have a responsibility to work for the success of the organization that issues them. It's up to you to sell the goods – even when you're not so sure you'd buy them yourself.

As a young actor, I participated in a new play series at a major regional repertory theater. In this kind of workshop atmosphere, actors play a dual role. During rehearsals, they're invited to critique each script and make suggestions for improving it. But once each play opens, they're expected to give their absolute all to performing it as it is written. One of the plays in the series, by a playwright who would go on to become quite well-known, had significant problems that all the actors recognized. We pleaded with the author and the director to address these problems, but both were blind to the flaws in the work.

Emotions ran high during rehearsals; there were moments of crisis and gloom. A mordant joke circulated among the actors: "How many playwrights does it take to change a light bulb? None – it doesn't need changing!" But when the curtain went up on opening night, did we go onstage and sulk? Did we "back off" from the script we were given or, even worse, try to sabotage it with poor performances? Of course not. We did everything we could, in every performance, to make the play succeed as the playwright created it. We left it to the audience to judge the work, because that's what actors owe to every playwright and every audience.

And yet. I understand that nobody wants to stand up and rave about a product they're afraid will fail, an initiative they think is wrong-headed, or a position they find flimsy. Clients sometimes take me aside and ask some very hard questions: What if I really don't believe in this product? What if I think this initiative is misguided? What if I know I'm simply covering for somebody else's mistakes? How can I sell this message – how am I supposed to survive this presentation – when I think it's a fraud?

Luckily, the issues are not often so black and white. When your convictions are at odds with what you're being asked to communicate, it's time to take stock. Rethink your position with an open mind. Make an effort to find out more about why the organization has embarked on an initiative you think is flawed, shipped a product you don't believe in, or taken a position you disagree with. Discuss the issues with someone you trust. Playing devil's advocate with colleagues is always a good way of probing for weak spots in your messaging and anticipating questions and objections. It can also help you overcome your own objections – by taking both a short- and a long-term view on an issue, identifying the strengths of a risky program, or empathizing with those who support a product or program you have doubts about.

Let's be realistic. Most jobs and careers involve at least a few occasions when you just have to take a deep breath and do your best. You can't always pick and choose and give support only to ideas and initiatives that meet with your personal approval. There may be times when you have to ask yourself: Can I get on board without compromising my fundamental beliefs or values? I've found that most times, in most circumstances, most people will be able to answer, "Yes."

If it's your job to communicate, it's your job to find your way to that "Yes" about what you are communicating. Then, on that foundation, it's your job to build a commitment to what you are communicating and why. Because only if you are committed will you be persuasive.

The Third Truth: *Victor or victim? That's up to you.*

When you're speaking or presenting in public, you have a choice: you can be a victor or a victim. What I want to emphasize is that it is a choice you make – or rather, a series of choices.

Staring at you from the page, this truth may seem obvious. But I've worked with hundreds of clients – some preparing for specific public speaking events, some devoting considerable time and effort to developing their "everyday" communication and leadership skills. Time and again, I've seen people make choices that set them up to be victims rather than victors when they stand in front of an audience and speak. And more often than not, they are unaware of those choices.

The baseline, of course, is confidence. Again, this may seem obvious, even banal. There's a saying that's been making the rounds – "Whether you believe you will succeed or you will fail, you are right." Sounds like the mother of all self-help mantras, doesn't it? And then there's our media culture, where sports are supremely important and we get to see athletes "up close and personal" – probably more than we would like. From boxers to baseball players, we get plenty of "psyching myself up," "finding the flow," or "getting into the head" of an opponent.

But strip away all the hype, and there's still plenty of truth in the clichés about confidence. Superior athletes and great competitors in every walk of life grasp it intuitively. Most of us have to learn it, and the bearing it has on our power of persuasion. It is this: The more confident you are, the better you will perform.

When you're confident in front of an audience, you're relaxed but alert. You breathe more deeply and evenly. Oxygen fills your lungs and flows freely to your muscles, giving you more vocal and physical energy, and to your brain, enabling you to think more clearly. In full command of all your resources as a speaker, you are capable of performing at your peak.

At the other extreme is what's called stage fright, which is actually a severe case of under-confidence. In a person afflicted with stage fright, breathing becomes rapid and shallow; the heart races and so does the mind. The person feels ill because he is. Physically and mentally debilitated, such a person doesn't have a chance of performing at his peak; just getting through the ordeal at hand is challenge enough.

In the third part of this book, "Learning Your Craft as a Communicator," I talk about being nervous (which is not unhealthy – far from it) and preparing your body and voice for speaking in public. What I want to do here is make you aware of some of most common choices every speaker must make – choices between victor and victim, choices that will either bolster or undermine your confidence.

Believe it or not, you choose whether or not to believe in your own message. How could anyone choose not to? I've seen it happen many times.

Sometimes the problem is being too smart. I find that my most intelligent, thoughtful, and informed clients are often harder on themselves and their message than they should be. They compulsively poke holes in their own arguments. They over-analyze the situation, the position they're taking or the announcement they're making, whatever. In the process they lose sight of the big picture. Knowing more than they can possibly communicate, they get hung up on what they're leaving out of their presentation and lose focus on what they want to say.

I've also worked with people who buy into negative perceptions about their company or industry or profession. People in technology who are troubled by the distrust of customers or competitors. People in healthcare who feel that, somehow, they are personally to blame for the costs and complexities of modern healthcare. People in pharmaceuticals who feel tainted by direct-to-consumer drug advertising.

If you're preparing for a speech or presentation and you catch yourself being too smart, too fastidious, too concerned about the shades of gray – stop. You're undercutting your confidence and setting yourself up to be a victim.

Don't dwell on the flaws or limitations of your company's new product or service. Instead, focus on the progress and innovation it represents, and the huge benefits to be reaped from this "breakthrough" and the improvements that are sure to follow.

Don't lose your way in a thicket of "on-the-other-hand," "yeah-but," and "what-if." The moment you start to hedge, your audience will start to tune out. Remember, people are there to listen to you. That makes you the expert. Of course you know more than you can – or should – explain. What your audience wants you to do is cut to the heart of the matter. (In the second part of this book, "Discovering and Developing Your Message," I put a great deal of emphasis on simplicity as the foundation of clarity, for you and your audience.)

Finally, as a public speaker, you will often have some very practical choices to make, both before and after you take the floor. These are victor-victim choices, too.

Victims agree to talk about issues or answer questions that are outside their expertise. Victims cut corners on preparation and rehearsals. Victims don't bother to visit the site of their presentation – the "set" for their performance – ahead of time; or if they do, they're too polite to ask that the room set-up be changed to improve sight lines or acoustics. Victims get flustered by microphones and unfamiliar equipment. Instead of making sure that everything is organized for their success, victims "let come what may," which only drives up the chances they will fail.

Instead of demanding the attention of every person in the room, victims allow audience members to talk, or scroll through e-mail on their PDAs, or check their voicemail.

You have rights when speaking to a group (summarized in "The Speaker's Bill of Rights" at the end of this chapter). You have the right to focus on subjects about which you are knowledgeable. You have the right to prepare and rehearse adequately. You have the right to a room configuration that helps you perform your best. You have the right to request that a 4-inch platform be placed behind the lectern so that, even at 5 feet 6 inches, you can see and be seen by the audience. You have the right to understand how to raise and lower the microphone, and to feel comfortable with all the other equipment you'll use in your presentation.

In short, you have the right to be successful. And you have the right to the undivided attention of your audience.

As I said at the beginning of these pages on victor-versus-victim, I've learned that most people are not conscious of the choices they make that set them up to be victims. They couldn't be; otherwise, they surely wouldn't cooperate in undermining their own cause. That's why awareness is essential. Once you're aware of the victor-victim choices, you can make sure that you always make the right choices as a speaker — the ones that set you up to succeed.

Exercise: Uncovering Your Passion

Your passion may lie deep inside. It may be difficult to articulate. But you must find it and give it voice to be successful. To uncover it, sit down with a trusted colleague or friend or turn on a tape recorder and answer these questions:

- Why is the work I'm doing important? Why does it matter to the world, and why does it matter to me?
- What do I love about what I'm doing? When I think back to a milestone achieved or a moment of triumph, how did I feel at the time? How do I feel about it now?
- When things are not going well, how do I feel? Why do I put up with the hassles and the headaches?
- What's at stake, for me and beyond me, short-term and over the long haul? What are the everyday rewards? What's the pot of gold at the end of the rainbow?

The Speaker's Bill of Rights

1. You have the right to be confident.
2. You have the right to succeed.
3. You have the right to speak about what you know best and to speak about what moves you.
4. You have a right to the time and resources you need to prepare and rehearse prior to a presentation.
5. You have a right to coaching and feedback as you prepare for a presentation.
6. You have the right to refuse last-minute changes and requests that will undermine your preparation and confidence.
7. You have the right to control the presentation environment. This includes (but is not limited to) the right to be comfortable with any technology that will be part of your presentation, to have the microphone at the proper height, and to ask for a glass of water.
8. You have the right to be heard. This includes the right to demand an audience's attention.
9. You have the right to pause to collect your thoughts, correct yourself, or repeat anything you think the audience might have missed
10. You have the right not to answer a question or respond to a comment.

Chapter 2
Listen Up

During my first year of formal training as a professional actor, the focus was not on how well students talked when we were on stage but on how well we listened. We would act out scenes together, and then the instructor would critique our "performances." I put that word in quotes because, in fact, we heard almost nothing about the way we had delivered our own lines; instead, we got extensive feedback on how well we had listened when the other actor was talking.

I'm sure I wasn't the only student asking himself, *This* is acting? But, though some egos got bruised along the way, eventually we absorbed the truth and importance of our instructor's approach. In theater parlance, we were learning that acting is the art of "being in the moment," and you simply can't do that if you don't listen to the other actors onstage. More fundamentally, we were learning that all communication is a transaction – a transaction between people – and what happens on the listening end is just as important as what happens on the talking end.

The power of persuasion is largely a matter of projecting who you are and what you want to say, clearly and forcefully, and most of this book focuses on that. But developing your listening skills is also an essential part of your preparation as a communicator. For one thing, preparation for a speech or presentation often involves gathering information from other people. With good listening skills, you will literally hear more when others talk, because good listening encourages good communication.

Just as important to your preparation, it's your job to learn what you can about the audience you're going to speak to. What do they expect to hear? What do they want to hear? What might engage them, challenge them, motivate them? "WIIFM" – short for "What's in it for me?" – is the siren song no audience can resist. But in order to create that seductive music, you have to be a good listener.

The Listening Tour

Most of my client engagements are about more than a single speech. They are about an extended communications campaign. Like any such effort, a communications campaign takes careful planning, thinking, and listening.

In undertaking such a campaign – even in preparing for a one-time presentation – you may think you know what your key objectives are. You may think you understand all the issues. But do you? Again, all communication is a transaction between speaker and listener. Your audience or audiences will bring their own ideas, thoughts, and feelings to every meeting, every presentation, every event.

Unless you understand their point of view, their concerns and prejudices and fears, their current levels of understanding and resistance regarding your objectives – unless you understand all of that, you can't plan a persuasive presentation, you can't craft effective messages, you can't even be sure that you've defined your objective correctly and completely.

That's why I urge my clients to go on a listening tour before preparing a presentation or planning a campaign. Internally, your listening tour may simply be a stroll through the work site to engage important people and find out about their current perceptions and concerns. Externally, it might mean more. A recent client took the listening tour exercise very seriously. New to his leadership position but slated to give a keynote address at an industry conference attended by his most important customers and partners, he actually got on the airplane and met with six of his most important constituents. When he returned from the trip, he had a whole new perspective on his keynote.

Listening Styles

To understand the importance of good listening – and what kind of listener you are – you can start by being aware of how other people listen. Two archetypes define the extremes of listening styles. Although most of us fall somewhere in between, we usually share at least some of the characteristics of both extremes, at least some of the time.

Withholders are the people who give back nothing – zero, zilch, nada – when you talk to them. They often sit with arms crossed, their expression blank if not slightly troubled. It's easy to feel that they're sitting in judgment of you – if they haven't already found you guilty! Speaking to them is like sending information into a black hole. We've all met withholders, probably more often than we'd like.

Some, I believe, are misguided by the belief that all communications are about power and status; in withholding, they've found their favorite intimidation technique. Others, I'm sure, don't engage in withholding on purpose; they simply come from a background that predisposed them to this kind of expressionless listening. And many people who aren't ordinarily withholders will retreat into this listening style in threatening or stressful situations.

Whatever their reasons, withholders make it tough on the rest of us. Their lack of response can be extremely frustrating and stressful; it can take us off our game, which is precisely what some withholders seem to have in mind. Our inner monologue goes wild: "Why is this interaction going so badly? Does he think I'm full of it? Do I have spinach in my teeth? Maybe if I try harder, or change my message, I can get some kind of response."

After an encounter with a withholder, it's easy to feel that you've failed miserably in gathering any meaningful information. That's why it's important to be able to identify a withholder when you deal with one – you'll know that your apparent failure to connect is not your fault. By sabotaging communications, withholders really shortchange nobody but themselves.

Clients often ask me how they should respond to this extreme style of listening. I suggest continual "checking" with withholders – that is, ask them frequently if they understand what you're saying, what they think of what you've said, if they agree or disagree, what they might add. It's also a good idea to turn some of your statements into questions that require a response. When you feel you can risk it, come right out and tell withholders that you need more feedback. Tell them that, because you're not sure what they're thinking, you're concerned that you're not communicating effectively.

If you think that you are a withholder, I strongly recommend that you make an effort to change your ways. Withholders aren't just poor listeners; they tend to be poor communicators as well. They get much less information, and much less help, from those they communicate with, and they often end up delivering the wrong message.

Gushers appear to think of listening as a vigorous physical challenge, a matter of continuous head nodding, endless "ums" and "ahs," and frequent interruptions. Maybe they believe that they're making it easier and more comfortable for us to communicate with them. But more often than not, their ostentatious, hyperactive manner of listening distracts us from communicating effectively. Continually interrupted, prevented from finishing a thought, even actively encouraged to go off course, we may find that talking with a gusher is even more unsettling than dealing with a withholder.

When you deal with gushers, it can be difficult to get them to minimize the affirmations. There just aren't many ways to tell people that they're being too nice. But you can get them to stop the interruptions. Tell them that you "really want to get this right" and their interruptions are causing you to lose your train of thought.

Ask them to wait to ask questions – even to jot down notes – so that you can engage in dialogue when you "finish laying out the background."

And if you think you are a gusher, take stock – you would do well to develop another style of listening. Just as the withholder's style may serve to elevate his or her status and authority, gushing is sure to do the opposite for you. During many executive coaching sessions, I've had to ask the client to back off on the gushing. Excessive nodding, prodding, and affirmation diminishes a person's authority. More likely than not, it will mark you as someone who is "not a leader."

Knowing your style is the key, so you can modulate it as necessary. Wherever each of us fits on the scale between withholders and gushers, we can borrow elements from both in order to become better listeners. Used in moderation, gushing with someone who needs encouragement will allow him or her to gain confidence, open up, and communicate more fully and more clearly. Conversely, some people we encounter need to feel that they have our complete focus in order to communicate well; they'll communicate better if we rein back our responses in the manner of the withholder.

Authentic Listening

On his way to a guaranteed laugh, one of my acting teachers once said, "The key to great acting is being truthful. *[pause]* And if you can fake that, you've got it made." The wisdom behind the joke is as true of listening as it is of talking. Faking genuine interest almost always backfires. But that doesn't mean you can't learn to listen well.

For some people, good listening comes naturally; they simply have a knack for listening in a caring and heartfelt manner, attuned not only to the words but also to the emotions of the speaker. For the rest of us, good listening requires focus, intention, and training – just as I and my fellow students learned in acting school. Every parent of young children knows that human beings decide when they want to listen (and when they don't). We can also control how we listen, which means we can ensure that we listen well. It just takes a bit of work – a combination of will, awareness, and technique.

In one of the most popular Power of Persuasion workshops, I engage groups in various listening games and exercises. In several of these activities, the paradox is how little there is to listen to. The exercises require people to use their bodies in the communication process; what gets everyone laughing and enjoying themselves – and makes them better, more aware listeners – is finding that their ears and their brains go where their bodies lead. Following is a summary of what these listening workshops demonstrate.

Body language speaks silently but eloquently; moment by moment, it express-es how well you are listening. Good listening requires body language that enhances rather than hampers the transaction between you and the person you are listening to. So it's important to be aware of productive and non-productive body language and to practice using those that serve you best. The basics include:

Do	Don't
Lean in slightly toward the speaker	Play the withholder
Keep an open posture	Sit back in judgment or cross your arms
Affirm by nodding your head occasionally	Fidget, tap your foot, click your pen, check your watch, and so forth

Eye contact is a crucial element of communication. This is what our parents were trying to teach us when they told us to "look the man in the eye." The matter is a little more complicated than our parents might have known. Cultural anthropologists have made us aware that there are marked cultural variations around the issue of eye contact. In an era of globalization, anyone who interacts face-to-face with people from non-Western societies has to be sensitive to those variations. Nevertheless, in North America the generally accepted practice is to engage the eyes of people you're talking to.

Yes, but how much eye contact is appropriate? I'm certainly not recommending you lock eyes with everyone you talk to. Anyone who has been subjected to this form of "listening" knows how uncomfortable it can be. On the other hand, the proverbial saying that the eyes are the window to the soul reminds us that people's eyes often tell us how they feel about what they're saying, and that's an important part of all communication.

My recommendation: Don't overthink the matter of eye contact. When listening to someone, simply engage his or her eyes enough to "check in and check up" – to let them know that you are engaged with them and to monitor how they feel about what they're saying.

You need to look into the eyes of people you want to persuade, if only because they need to look into yours. When first taking the stage for a presentation, or as soon as you're introduced, it's important to look at the audience. Avoid the pitfall of hiding your eyes, whether because you're nervous or shy or because you "just have to check your notes." You'll be more effective – and in fact, you will gain confidence – if you take a few moments to look out and make eye contact with the audience before you begin speaking. Search for someone you know or a friendly face. While you're looking out at them, your audience will get a good look at you – and they'll start to feel that they know you. In those few critical moments, the all-important connection between you and them will begin to form.

Checking to make sure we've heard correctly is an excellent way to ensure we're listening carefully. To check, use simple phrases like "So what I'm hearing you say is …" or "Let me be sure that I understand you …" This gives others the chance to confirm or correct your understanding of what they're saying and what they want. It also assures them that you are a good listener, and that makes them want to listen to you.

Empathetic Listening and Asking the "Why" Questions

Listening happens on many levels. Many people listen simply for the facts, focusing on what is being said in its literal detail. But some people have a special talent for what I call empathetic listening: they're able to connect not just with what someone is saying but also with how the speaker feels about what he or she is saying. Then there are those who ask themselves a series of "why" questions while they listen: *"Why is this person saying that?… What's really going on here?… What's behind that comment?… What's the real story?"*

Empathetic listeners and people who listen with the "why" questions working in the background of their minds are not necessarily "better" listeners. But they often glean information from their interactions that others do not – nuances of fact or feeling that can open up whole new perspectives on events or issues, as well as hidden agendas, unspoken resistance, and other obstacles to progress or change.

When you're lucky enough to run into empathetic listeners, observe them closely and try to emulate their techniques – provided you can do so genuinely. And try to cultivate the habit of asking "why" questions when listening to others. These two listening styles may not be "better" than yours, but they can make you a more effective listener.

Listening While Presenting

Listening is a critical skill during interactive presentations. Panel discussions, conferences, team meetings during which you are a presenter, sessions with the media, and so forth – forums like these require you to listen as well as speak. And how well you listen informs how well and how persuasively you speak.

Even when you're behind the podium and doing all the talking, you must listen to your audience. Just as it is for actors on stage, listening is the most effective means we have of conveying genuine interest in other people. And it is vital to convey genuine interest in those you wish to persuade. It will enable you to command their attention with a presentation energy that says, "I care about what you are hearing and right now, in this moment, I am listening to and attentive to your reaction."

Even as you're talking to them, you have to be alert to the things your audience is telling you. Think of it as a form of instant polling that will help you make course corrections in your presentation on the fly. We've all sat through presentations, from classes to conferences, where some misguided speaker droned on and on, as the shuffling of feet and paper, the shifting in seats and clearing of throats grew toward a crescendo. Remember how embarrassed you felt for that speaker, or how disdainful? An audience will tell you when you need to move on to a new topic, change your position on the stage, add variety to your vocal style – anything to recapture their attention. Later chapters in this book introduce various ways to do that. But in order to know when to put those techniques in action – Listen up!

Listening Exercise

It's best to have a stopwatch when doing this exercise.

Sit with a partner and have him or her answer, in 5 to 7 minutes, the following questions about a current or planned communications campaign:

- What's the "lay of the land" – that is, the situation of the organization you seek to influence?
- What are the major issues you need to address or initiatives you need to drive through your communications campaign?
- What are the major obstacles to success?
- How do you plan to overcome those obstacles?

Next, in 2 or 3 minutes, play back to your partner the key elements of what you heard, then ask them how completely and accurately you heard what you were told.

If your partner is willing, switch roles. This exercise can serve both of you in two ways: it can help you develop your listening skills, and it can also give you an opportunity to plan and develop a communications campaign.

Chapter 3
The Vision Thing

vi-sion n. 1. The sense of sight: eyesight.
2. Unusual discernment; intelligent foresight: a leader of vision.

It's no accident that we describe a person with vision as both inspired and inspiring. That's what vision does: it breathes the power of persuasion into the person who gives voice to it, and the force of conviction into the people who hear.

But, like charisma, vision is elusive or intimidating or both. Skeptics may think of vision as a cliché, or as something pompous or flaky or phony (at least until they encounter someone who has it). The skeptics' view, I suspect, is just sour grapes. For them as for many of us, vision is one of those "grand" abilities that seems beyond our abilities – or our responsibilities. We recognize its extraordinary power when we experience it in others. But if we're asked to describe our own vision, we start to squirm.

"Martin Luther King had vision – that's what made him great," we're likely to think. "The CEO has vision – that's why she's the CEO. But *me* – with a vision? Anything I came up with would just sound hollow, and I'd look like a fool."

But vision is not beyond any of us, and part of your preparation as a speaker or presenter is to cultivate a vision of your own. Whether you're cynical about "the vision thing" or intimidated by some inflated notion about what vision is and who has it, I suggest you stick a pin in your idea of vision, let some of the air out of it, and shrink it down to everyday size. Then start looking around. The elements of a coherent, compelling vision lie all around you, whatever your profession or position.

Looking Far and Near

To have vision – to see – you have to open your eyes and look. You have to look far and you have to look near. Hunkered down as we are in the day-to-day of our jobs, it's all too easy for most of us, most of the time, to lose sight of "the big picture." Leaders are people who make it a regular practice to raise their heads and scan the horizon. There, after all, is where the big picture – ideas, trends, possibilities – is to be seen.

Drilling down can be just as important as looking around, because the full meaning and import of things are rarely to be found on the surface. Think of yourself as a detective sifting the evidence. Get used to asking yourself and others, "What's *really* going on here, and why?" This habit of mind, also typical of leaders, will give you a depth of understanding that goes beneath the surface – the kind of insight a compelling vision is built on.

Insight over Information

Authority, vision, leadership: when speaking in public, none of these is a matter of showing off how much you know, but of how much you understand. We've all sat through presentations made up of one PowerPoint slide after another, all crammed with "facts," while the speaker plodded along in a tedious recitation of information we could just as easily have read in the printed hand-out. Who wants to listen to a data download or be overwhelmed by a fire hose of information?

Information is important. Writing teachers speak of the power of *illustrative details* – the *scarlet* dress, the *million-dollar* heist, the *shudder* of the ship. In an effective speech or presentation, facts and data serve as illustrative details: they enrich the "story," make it vivid, and convince us that it is true. But they are not the story itself.

Every audience wants to hear more than a recitation of the facts; they want to hear *what you make of the facts*. It's not enough to tell them "the data is trending in this or that direction" – they want to hear your insights about *why* and *what it all means*. Anyone can tell us what's happening. An insightful, persuasive speaker – one that we want to listen to and agree with – tells us why. *That* is the vision thing.

Dare to Predict

There is prodigious power in prediction. In my work, I get many chances to watch people as they listen to a speaker, and I have seen it again and again: an audience will literally lean forward in their seats when a speaker says something like "By this time next year, we'll see that …" or "I believe that five years from now …." No wonder the leaders I work with who capture the most attention are the ones who dare to put predictions into their presentations.

After all, when you make a prediction, what's the worst thing that can happen? You'll be wrong. By then, chances are that no one will remember your prediction. Besides, there are worse things than being wrong. When I work with leaders, I advise them that there's far more downside risk in being seen as someone who has no idea, or is afraid to say, what the future holds.

What trends and issues are going to drive your industry in the next two years or three or five? How will behavior change with the introduction of your company's new innovation? What will the jury conclude when you've finished presenting the evidence? How will both employees' and customers' lives be different after this reorganization? Dare to predict. If you've done your homework and thought through the facts and issues, you'll probably be right. In the meantime, you'll surely be regarded by your audience as a person with a strong point of view.

History as the Gateway to the Future

As expressed by the dictionary definition at the head of this chapter, vision is a matter of "intelligent foresight." That's why daring to predict the future is important. But vision – and the wherewithal to predict the future – often rests on knowing and understanding the past.

For decades, Paul Saffo has been the director of the renowned Institute for the Future in Menlo Park, California. By forecasting technological, demographic, and business trends, the non-profit Institute helps companies plan for the future, and it has worked for and won the trust of major businesses and government agencies around the world, including 3M, Intel, and the U.S. Postal Service. Understandably, the press likes to refer to Mr. Saffo as a "futurist." But it's a label he dislikes. As he has said, the secret of his success is not that he is a futurist but that he is a historian. His forecasting rests on his ability to recognize and understand the constants, not the novelties, in the evolution of technology, industry, and society.

If you want to impress an audience as a person of vision, you could do worse than follow Paul Saffo's example. Again, any time you speak or present in public, you are setting yourself up as an authority. You owe it to yourself as well as your audience to know what you're talking about, and that includes the history of your business or industry, the technical innovations that led to your new product, the background of the issues in your profession or field that you want to resolve.

Only by understanding the past will you really be qualified to recognize, much less announce, the milestones of today or the promises of the future. Just as the dictionary says, vision is *intelligent* – which means, among other things, *informed* – foresight.

Vision and Storytelling

To create and communicate a compelling vision, one of the best approaches you can take is to tell the story of the future. This is why I take many clients through a process I call *aspirational storytelling*. While storytelling as a multi-purpose technique is discussed in detail in Chapter 7, I introduce aspirational storytelling here because it's a such a great way to create a vision and put it into words.

The goal of aspirational storytelling is to describe what life will look like and feel like, in vivid and specific detail, when your idea, your strategy, or your mission has come to fruition. For example, you might describe a day in the life of your customers as they use, experience, and benefit from your product. Or tell the story of a week in the life of your management team once they've come together around a plan for organizational growth and development.

Your story of the future can take many forms. Martin Luther King, Jr's classic "I have a dream" speech is a tried and true model. Another compelling approach is to tell your story from the point of view of the future, looking back on the present moment as if it were the past: "Back in 2008 we made three key decisions, and on that foundation we have built the company that dominates our industry today ..."

Some examples: In healthcare, clients have used aspirational storytelling to paint a picture of a clinic visit made more effective and efficient for doctors, nurses, and patients by automated medical records. PR agencies have created the story of a world where clients deftly navigate difficult political waters, then revealed what was going on behind the scenes to facilitate that success. Technology executives have produced a detailed "day in the life" scenario for a family using a portable mobile phone and media player to take their music, movies, and games with them as they hike into the mountains. In finance, I've listened as clients describe what life will be like when Sarbanes-Oxley compliance is fully integrated into the financial systems of large organizations.

Aspirational storytelling can facilitate more than message development — far more. It often serves as a form of strategic planning, because you can't describe a future of success without explaining how you will create that success. For leaders and management teams, painting a picture of the future is often the catalyst for coming to grips with what the organization must do to get there. That's why, when I coach leaders, I often begin with aspirational storytelling. But again, vision is not for leaders only. A magical elixir compounded of insight, aspiration, and determination, vision can make leaders of us all.

Part II:
Discovering and Developing Your Message

Introduction

With the right attitude, a visceral connection with your mission, good listening skills, and a vision to share, you have a solid foundation for building and delivering a compelling presentation. In this part of you'll learn some reliable methods for discovering and developing your message, powerful techniques for driving your message home, and ways of structuring a presentation that will command your audience's attention from start to finish.

The Importance of Method in Message Development

Many organizations have some kind of process for preparing a presentation, even if it's just "this person writes the PowerPoints, and that person makes them look good." But when I started out as a coach and consultant, I was surprised at how few clients have any kind of disciplined method for executing the most fundamental task: figuring out what they want and need to say. Fewer still have a grasp of the rhetorical and structural tools that make messages forceful to the ear and memorable in the mind.

That's what the techniques presented here are for. Chapters 4 and 5 describe methods for discovering and then developing your message. Chapters 6 and 7 show you how to use two of the most fundamental – and most effective – rhetorical tools available to any speaker. Finally, Chapter 8 outlines what I believe is the most effective structure for business and professional presentations.

The Spoken Word Is King

We tend to think of talking as a "lesser" form of communication. After all, our days are filled with conversation, but occasions for "formal" speaking are few and far between. For communications, such as those in business and professional life, we may tend to believe that it's necessary to "put it in writing." There's no question that the printed word has a certain authority. And writing is often an essential means both to discovering what we think and to organizing our thoughts.

So why do I say that the spoken word is king?

Think about your desk and your computer desktop at work. If you're like most people, you're awash in documents of all kinds, sent to you by people who want to inform or influence you, solicit your ideas or share their own. Think, too, how many e-mails you send every week, how many plans, proposals, and reports you write in a month or a year.

And then consider all the times you've distributed a written plan or proposal – even something as simple as an agenda – prior to a meeting. The idea is that the attendees will review the document before they attend, right? But as the meeting gets underway, you soon come to the unsettling conclusion that Or, if you've ever given a media interview, think about what got quoted in the story. It wasn't the background documents you gave to the reporters to educate and inform them – it's what you said during the interview that got into print.

The fact is, people just don't read much anymore. Chances are, what you say about a plan, a proposal, or a report is going to have far more influence than the document itself.

And yet, even when getting ready for a presentation, many people spend the lion's share of their preparation time on the written word – creating background documents, outlining what they want to cover, writing PowerPoint slides. They spend little time, even no time at all, actually saying out loud what they want to say when the moment comes that they're on their feet and everyone is looking at them expectantly. They go into battle like a soldier who's spent the night before polishing his boots instead of cleaning his rifle.

As you go about discovering and developing your message, it's essential that you use the medium you will use to present it: the spoken word. That means everything you will say in your presentation before you commit it to paper or PowerPoint.

Chapter 4
Discovering Your Message

Before you can develop a presentation, write a speech, or plan a high-stakes meeting, you have to know what your message is – just as you have to have a pattern to weave a rug, a design to build a building, or a plan to put a man on the moon.

Why are you summoning the power of persuasion? Unless you're Garrison Keillor or Jerry Seinfeld, you're not talking to people for their amusement (or your own). You're out to accomplish something. *You need to solve a problem.* You can't come up with a solution until you have a complete, detailed understanding of the problem.

So the first step is to step back.

Set the Context: Who? When? Where?

Business and marketing people often call it situational analysis. I call it setting the context. All communications take place in a context, made up of several elements. Because these circumstances will influence how you will be *heard*, you must take them into account as you develop what you plan to *say*. Before you jump into content, you must understand context. Sometimes you may be able to do that by asking one big question: What is the context? More often, it's a matter of asking and answering a series of little questions.

As any writer will tell you, the fundamental rule of communication is to think about your audience first, last, and always. *Who* are you talking to and trying to persuade?

That's not one question but many. You should try to answer *all the questions you can* about the audience you'll be presenting to – questions such as these:

- What's their status? Leaders, executives, middle managers, rank-and-file? Colleagues, customers, employees?

- How do they think and how do they learn? Are they technical people, visual people, numbers people?
- What's their point of view on the issues you plan to address?
- What do they *expect* to hear? What do they *want* to hear? What do they *need* to hear?
- Who are you to them, and how will that influence the way they listen to you?

That is, what do they know about you? What do they think and feel about you?

Next question: When are you presenting? By this, I don't just mean what day and time you're scheduled to speak (although the time of day can affect both your energy and your audience's attention span, which is why mornings are best for presentations). More important is the "virtual" when:

- When in the product lifecycle or sales process?
- When in the history of your relationship with the audience?
- When in your budget cycle or theirs?
- When in the history of your organization or industry?

The more such *When?* questions you can ask and answer, the better.

Next question: *Where* is the presentation taking place? This too is less a question of physical space than "virtual" space. Will you be in hostile territory – for example, at a tradeshow or analysts' meeting where you might be regarded as a competitor, an upstart, an unknown quantity? Or in friendly territory – for example, at a client conference or developers' forum where you're known as a trusted partner or likable underdog?

Of course, the *where* of your presentation is a physical matter, too. If you know what kind of facility or room you'll be presenting in – large or small, on a stage or not, with what kind of AV equipment, and so forth – you have to think about how that might affect your options for presenting your message and the audience's expectations.

The last but far from the least important question you must ask about the context of your presentation is this: What is *really* going on here?

In drama and literature, this is called the *subtext* – what the characters really want, what they really mean or think as opposed to their words and actions. Business, professional, and organizational life often has subtext, too, with various layers of meaning lurking beneath the surface – politics, unspoken agendas, unacknowledged fears, interpersonal dynamics and tensions, unresolved issues from past interactions, scores to settle, and so forth. Chances are, some such not-so-hidden layers of meaning surround the speech, presentation, or meeting you're planning for. You absolutely must take them into account in developing your message.

Assess the Opportunities and Risks

Problem-solving usually involves risks as well as opportunities. Most of my clients in business and professional life know this. Even so, I usually advise them to think and *talk* through the opportunities and risks involved in the presentation, meeting, or communication campaign they're preparing for.

Doing so serves several purposes. By laying out what's at stake, you force yourself to define how you'll measure the success of your presentation. By describing what that success will mean, you clarify your goals. And by focusing your eyes on the prize, you sharpen your motivation.

To assess the opportunities, ask yourself these questions:
- What are your hopes and dreams for this presentation?
- What's the upside? List the specific results and benefits you'll see if everything goes perfectly and you really knock the socks off your audience.
- What's the ideal overall outcome – for your organization, your product or project, your brand, your personal reputation?

To assess the risks, ask yourself these questions:
- If your presentation goes poorly, what's the cost?
- Where will that leave your product or initiative, your brand, your organization, your personal reputation?
- What kind of "damage control" will you have to do to offset the consequences if you botch this opportunity? How much time and what resources will such an effort require?

Define Your Objective

You've looked at the context from all the angles, and you've probably splashed some cold water in your face with an honest assessment of the opportunities and risks. Now you're ready to start moving toward developing your message.

Start with the most basic definition of your objective. What do you want to accomplish?

Great speeches and effective presentations drive people to *action*. That's why a great way to define your objective is to ask yourself what you want your audience to *do* when you've finished talking to them. Some examples:

I want them to sign up to be organ donors.
I want them to ask for a meeting so we can discuss having my law firm represent them.

I want them to volunteer to join the next round of funding for my start-up.

I want them to understand how our software application can change their medical practice and to ask for an onsite demo.

I want them to acknowledge the need for this important resource and ask me for a budget proposal.

Having a strong objective is essential to your success as a persuader. In fact, I'll go so far as to say that once you know what you want, you are well on your way to getting it.

You may have heard of the Stanislavski system of acting. According to this system, every character in a drama has a central desire or objective (often called the *motivation*) that drives him or her in each scene, as well as a "super objective" for the entire play. An actor must never set foot on the stage without knowing what his or her character *wants*.

Just as all human feeling and behavior is driven by desire, the authentic portrayal of feeling and behavior must be rooted in desire as well. And of course, it is each character's pursuit of his or her objective, coming into conflict with external forces – including other characters in pursuit of *their* objectives – that creates and energizes the drama.

I urge my clients to operate according to Stanislavski's principles when approaching a presentation, speech, or high-stakes meeting. By defining a clear, strong objective, you'll improve your "performance" in several ways. You'll sharpen your focus on your desire to persuade. You'll become more intent on your audience – *their* needs, desires, and doubts, and your need to connect with them. You'll feel the urgency of wanting them to do whatever it is you want them to do, and you'll communicate that urgency.

Anticipate the Obstacles – and the Tough Questions

The Stanislavski system, with its emphasis on motivation and conflict, carries over into the next crucial step in the message discovery process. Like an actor preparing to play a character in a drama, you have defined your objective. You know what you want. Now you must look ahead to the conflict. You must ask yourself what, and who, is in your way.

In my experience, most of the obstacles you can anticipate exist, so to speak, in the minds of your audience. What will they question, doubt, disagree with, or reject – and why? Pay attention to the *type* of each such obstacle – its character, if you will – because different kinds of obstacles demand different approaches to overcoming them.

- Will you face obstacles of understanding? These are the easiest to overcome, provided you take the time (which means having the patience) to educate your audience by explaining what they may not know or don't understand.

- Will fears – of risk, change, the unknown – keep your audience from hearing, believing, or accepting what you say? Fear is a formidable adversary, especially when it's hidden, as it often is; how will you bring it out into the light and overcome it?
- Are you going up against prejudice, bias, or a competitor's campaign of misinformation? In other words, does your audience harbor ideas or beliefs – whether fair or unfair – that you'll have to rebut, disprove, or dislodge before you can "sell" your ideas or proposals?
- Is there a lack of urgency in the air? Do people generally agree with you but only if you don't ask them to take action – to change – now?

An excellent technique for identifying obstacles is to anticipate tough questions your audience might ask. In Chapter 12, "Winning Q&A," I discuss techniques for dealing with difficult questions (and difficult questioners). But it's never too early to consider the toughest questions you're likely to hear after you've finished your presentation. In fact, the message development process is an ideal time to start.

By anticipating the tough questions at an early stage, you can often build the answers into the body of your presentation. List five questions you'd rather not have to answer; I promise that you'll see five issues you *will* have to address sooner or later, and it should probably be sooner.

For Each Obstacle, Define a Key Message

At this stage, the obstacles to achieving your objective are not your enemies. They are your allies. They are the key to discovering what you want and need to say when you "take the stage."

By identifying obstacles and anticipating tough questions, you have broken down your objective into a set of tasks for your presentation. Now, your challenge is to turn every "Why?" or "What do you mean?" into an "I understand" … every unspoken "I'm afraid" into an outspoken "That's worth the effort or risk" … every uninformed or misinformed or timid "No" into a committed, heart-felt "Yes." In other words, each obstacle defines a key message for your presentation.

Two Examples

To illustrate the process of going from objective to obstacles to key messages, here I offer two examples from my experience.

Example 1: A company leader plans a high-stakes strategy session with her senior management team.

I worked with the leader of a health food company as she prepared for a strategic planning session with the company's senior management team. Better than anyone, she knew this would be a crucial moment for the company. She also knew that the session, which she was to open with a presentation, would be a crucial moment – a career-changing moment, one way or the other – for *her*.

The situation was this: The company's early success was based on consistently high levels of satisfaction among retail customers: people simply loved the company's products. But success and rapid growth had undermined some crucial quality control measures and diluted customer service efforts, and customer satisfaction levels were eroding. Meanwhile, the company faced ferocious new competition from larger, long-term players in the foodstuffs industry.

My client had a plan for the company, involving some drastic changes in its infrastructure, focus, and culture. She had a plan for the company, but that didn't mean she had a plan for her presentation. She knew she'd have to do much more than simply describe her proposals and leave the room.

I suggested that she start by defining her objective, focusing on the audience. This is what she came up with:

> *I want them to pledge "bet your career" support for a new*
> *company strategy focused on customer service and based on*
> *a culture of "disciplined entrepreneurship."*

This objective had multiple levels, and it left some important ideas undeveloped, but that was OK. It defined what she wanted her audience to *do* in no uncertain terms.

Next, we worked together on anticipating the obstacles. For her, this was a matter of listing the reasons her management team might resist the plan or withhold the complete commitment that she wanted from every one of them. Here's what she came up with:

- Most of them don't appreciate how much our customer satisfaction levels have eroded or how much that erosion has cost us in market share and reputation.
- They probably don't realize how rapidly market conditions are changing, and they may not appreciate the threat posed by our competitors.
- They're not familiar with available customer service software solutions designed to address the problems we have.
- They can be expected to feel threatened by the idea of retraining around new software.
- They can be expected to feel even more threatened by a new, company-wide emphasis on measuring customer satisfaction and rewarding ourselves and employees according to success in that area.

The first three were obstacles of understanding, and the last two combined a fear of change and an inadequate understanding of the rationale for it.

Based on her list of obstacles, my client was ready to create a list of key messages — the ideas she knew she would have to explain, clarify, and sell in order to persuade her audience that her plan for the company was the right one:

- By straying from our core strength — customer service and satisfaction — we have lowered our guard against the sleeping giants who are gearing up to compete ferociously with us.
- Our success, if not our survival, demands that we address our customer satisfaction problems *now*.
- To solve these problems, we must invest in a new customer service software solution and train everyone to use it.
- Software alone won't solve our problems. We must also refocus on customer satisfaction by monitoring and measuring our success in that area — and rewarding ourselves and our employees accordingly.
- At the same time, we must not become overly cautious as individuals or as a company. Bold entrepreneurship has been a key ingredient of our success. Now we need to create a culture of "disciplined entrepreneur ship," encouraging new ideas and initiatives that serve our customer-centric goals.
- The money we invest in this plan will be recovered within the first 16 months after the plan is in place.

Note that this leader did not end up with a strict point-by-point correspondence between her lists of obstacles and messages. The message discovery process is not that tidy, nor should it be. Most of the time, you'll probably come up with a whole laundry list of key messages. In their early form, your key messages may also be longer and more complex than the examples I've described here. Not to worry. In the next chapter, you'll find techniques for sharpening the focus of your messaging.

Example 2: The president of a nonprofit institution develops a fund-raising speech.

Together with a speechwriter, I worked with the president of a religious studies consortium to develop a fundraising speech. The objective was simple and clear:

I want them to contribute money to the consortium.

But in a briefing with the president and his staff, we identified a number of formidable obstacles.

Persuading people to give money to your nonprofit organization is a tricky business. Beyond making sure that your audience understands what you do and why it matters, you have to give them that all-important sense of "what's in it for me." And you have to make them feel a sense of *urgency* about your mission or your cause; otherwise, it's all too easy for them to go away and forget about you.

A museum or arts organization can boast about its programs and performances and offer perks like special events and priority access for donors. A medical foundation or relief organization can point to the lives it saves or the people it helps. But for an academic institution like the one I was working with, which is devoted to advanced education and research in a wide range of religions, the challenges are more daunting.

We listed the obstacles in the form of questions that would have to be addressed at least implicitly in the speech:

- What is the consortium? What does it do? What does it stand for?
- As an academic institution, isn't the consortium something of an "ivory tower?" What does it have to do with "real-world" problems – or solutions to those problems?
- I'm a Catholic/Lutheran/Jew/Buddhist/Muslim/etc. Why should I support the consortium instead of an institution associated with my own faith?
- The consortium has been around for a long time and is well-established; why does it need or merit my support now?
- The consortium was founded in the 1960s and is associated with a university known for its liberalism. If it has a political agenda I disagree with, why should I support it?

Clearly, some of these questions represented basic obstacles of understanding; others were more complicated. Note, in particular, that the last was one of those issues that lurks below the surface, one of those questions of "What's really going on here?" that I mentioned earlier in this chapter.

Based on these questions, we formulated the following key messages:

- Today it seems that people are more divided than ever by religious differences. From urgent debates in medicine, law, and education to bigotry and fanaticism, religious issues and conflicts plague our communities, our society, and the nations of the world.
- Through its unique mission – fostering advanced religious research and training in an interfaith environment – the consortium promotes dialogue and understanding among peoples and cultures of different religions.

- The consortium attracts unique individuals and prepares them for leadership not only in religious and academic institutions but beyond, in service to their communities, society, and the world.
- The consortium has no political agenda except to rescue religious thought and discourse from the shrill rhetoric and polarizing politics that exploit religious issues for partisan purposes.
- The consortium is a place where religion meets the world, and the training, commitment, and service of our graduates make the world a better place.

In this instance, framing the questions that could be expected to form in the minds of the audience was somewhat speculative. After all, this was to be a stump speech, something that the president of the consortium could use with various audiences. So the audience was considerably more of an unknown quantity than the health food company leader faced in her high-stakes meeting with her own senior management team. And yet the technique – anticipate the obstacles, then decide what you need to say to overcome them – worked just as effectively to discover and define the messaging foundation for the fundraising speech.

The Importance of Discovery

Sometimes I run into clients who resist the idea of discovering their messages. They feel quite sure that they know what they want to say, and they don't see any point in taking the time to go over it or delve into it. In the end, these clients profit from the message discovery process every bit as much as – and sometimes more than – those who start out with only vague ideas of what they want to say.

In my experience, effective leaders invest substantial time and energy in message discovery. Often, this is because they look beyond the event they're preparing for. They may be plotting a new course for their organization, like the health food executive. They may be kicking off an extended communications campaign, like the president of the religious studies consortium. Or they may be formulating an entire strategy for their enterprise, like one of the savviest clients with whom I've worked.

Every other year, this CEO hosted a three-day conference for his biggest customers and partners – a very important event for his $350 million business. Together with a speechwriter, I had the privilege of working with him on his keynote address for this event a couple of times.

At our kickoff meeting the second time around, the "briefing" we expected from this executive wandered far and wide. He speculated and theorized, mused and digressed, suggested ideas and tested ideas and rejected ideas – including some he had just suggested. The speechwriter tried to take notes, but pretty much gave up after a while (he was taping the discussion, anyway). Meanwhile, I was at the white board, trying to get down what I thought I was hearing and make some sort of order out of it. It wasn't a pretty picture. But it was teeming with ideas.

After a couple of hours we took a break, and when the client had left the room, the speechwriter turned to me in dismay. "I'm surprised he's so unprepared," he said of our client. "He seems to have no idea what he wants to say! What's the matter with him?"

I had known the client long enough to understand what he was up to. "We're not simply developing his speech for the conference," I explained. "He's using the speech to think through his plans for the business over the next two years." How did I know this? For one thing, each time he returned from the customer conference, the first thing he did was deliver his keynote address to his own employees.

Like great plays, compelling messages "have legs," as we say in the theater. They can carry you far beyond the speech, presentation, or high-stakes meeting you're preparing for. Propagated through an organization, elaborated for various audiences, media, and events, they can become a campaign, a strategy, a recipe for success. But, just like good plays, great messages take time and effort to discover and develop.

Exercise: Discovering Your Message

Consider a presentation you have coming up, or one you expect to make (or would like to make) in the more distant future. Give yourself 20 minutes to work your way through the following questions. By the end of this exercise, you'll not only "own" this technique for message discovery – you'll also have a blueprint of your presentation's key messaging.

Set the Context: Who? When? Where?

Who is your audience? Answer all the questions you can about them, including what they know and think about you (personally, as a leader or teacher, as the representative of a company or brand, etc.) and how that might prejudice or influence their response to you.

When are you presenting? What time of day? More important, when in the history of your relationship with the audience? When in the budget cycle, the sales process, the merger, the history of your initiative, etc.?

Where is the presentation taking place? In hostile, neutral, or friendly territory? In what kind of space (a conference room, an auditorium, or something in between) and with what kind of equipment (a stage and/or podium, A/V equipment, etc.).

Assess the Opportunities and Risks

What are the opportunities you hope to exploit with this presentation? List the results you'll achieve if the presentation goes well – immediately, within one month, six months, a year. How will a successful presentation enhance your personal reputation, your company's fortunes, or your brand?

What's at risk if your presentation goes poorly? Will your product fail … your initiative stall … your personal reputation, your company's fortunes, or your brand suffer? What will it cost – in time, money, lost opportunities – to recover?

Objective

What exactly do you want from your audience? More specifically, what do you want them to *do*? State your objective in an active sentence: *I want them to _____ .*

Obstacles and Tough Questions

List the obstacles to achieving your objective. Add five questions you don't want to answer.

Messages

List the key messages you have to get across in order to overcome the obstacles, answer the tough questions, and achieve your objective.

Chapter 5
Refining Your Message

After going through the discovery process described in the previous chapter, you'll probably end up with something of a laundry list of messages. That's OK – in fact, that's what you should end up with at the end of the discovery process. The point is to tease out everything you think you want to say or need to say based on your objective, the obstacles to achieving that objective, and the context and audience for your presentation.

That's the beginning of the message development process, but it's far from the end. During discovery you define your messages. Next, you have to refine them. Here again the analogy to writing is apt. Just as you must painstakingly draft, redraft, and edit a written document to make it as effective and persuasive as it can be, you have do to the same with any oral presentation.

By bringing up the analogy to writing, I do not mean to suggest that at this stage you are *outlining* your presentation. This chapter and the process it describes are not about structuring a presentation – that comes later. The objective here is to focus your thinking, your ideas, and your language on the goal you want to achieve, the ideas you want your audience to remember, the thing or things you want them to do.

Reduce the Sauce

Your first task is to take each important message and condense it to its core, its most powerful but complete essence. I call this *reducing the sauce*.

If you've ever made a risotto or created a fine bordelaise or similar sauce, you'll understand the point of my analogy: less is more. In cooking, a sauce acquires complexity, subtlety, depth, and power as it's reduced – until the critical moment when it reaches perfection. By the same token, a cook can weaken or spoil a sauce by reducing it *too much*.

The same is true of a spoken message. You have to go through a process of reducing the sauce to maximize the persuasive power of a message without sacrificing its clarity and completeness.

Returning to an example used in the previous chapter, consider the first message the health food company leader arrived at during her discovery process:

> *By straying from our core strength, we have awakened*
> *sleeping giants who are gearing up to compete ferociously*
> *with us.*

While it's dramatic and vivid – "watch out for those sleeping giants!" – in this form, the message is long and cumbersome. In fact, it sounds suspiciously like *two* messages:

> *We have strayed from our core strength.*

and

> *We have awakened sleeping giants who are gearing up*
> *to compete ferociously with us.*

The second idea is a consequence of the first. To reduce the sauce, my client focused on the first idea. But something was missing – just what was the core strength she was talking about? That, of course, had found its way into other messages on her list. "Customer service" was the seasoning she needed to add to the sauce while reducing it:

> *We have strayed from our core strength: customer service.*

This formulation was missing the element of "so what?" – the sense of what was at stake – conveyed by the threat of the "sleeping giants." So she experimented with ways of restoring that element, enriching the sauce while reducing it. Eventually, she arrived at this:

> *Where we used to be strong, in customer service,*
> *we are now weak – and vulnerable.*

This was short, complete, dramatic, memorable – in a word, powerful. It also gave my client a foundation to build on as she took the other messages on her list, reduced the sauce with each one, and put them together to build her case for reinventing the company through "disciplined entrepreneurship."

Reducing the sauce is a process of trial and error, experimentation, iteration and reiteration. The idea is to try out various words and phrases, formulations, and approaches for making each key point. But remember: the overarching goal is to reduce each message to its essence. Doing that will force you to be clearer, more concise, more direct, more persuasive.

As a rule, shorter is better, but there are limits to this rule. Like sentences, messages come in various forms: simple, compound, complex, and compound-complex. As with a risotto, you can spoil a message by going too far with your reduction. Fortunately, when you're preparing a presentation, you can always go back to a previous iteration, or restore a word or an idea, to save the sauce.

Exercise: Reduce the Sauce

1. Select one of the messages you arrived at through the discovery process.

2. Voice the message: Saying it out loud each time, try as many variations as you need to until you have phrased it as clearly and completely as you can.

3. With a stopwatch in hand, time yourself as you speak the message out loud. Now try to speak the message in half the time – not by talking faster but by reducing the number of ideas it contains and the number and length of the words you employ to express those ideas.

4. Repeat and reiterate the message – experiment – until you believe you can reduce it no further without making it unclear or meaningless.

5. Now, do the same with the rest of the messages you arrived at during your discovery process.

The Magic of Three

From the seven days of creation to *The Seven Habits of Highly Effective People,* seven is a number that has always captivated the human intellect and imagination. Apparently, seven is also the capacity of the human memory. For example, I've read that the basic paradigm for telephone numbers – 123-4567 – is based on the fact that the average person is capable of reliably remembering a sequence of seven digits and no more.

Maybe it's the supposed magic of seven that inspired the many clients I've worked with who wanted to base their presentations on seven messages. Without exception, I have discouraged them from doing so.

A friend of mine once told me about an executive speech he attended on "seven secrets to success" in the grocery business. As they left the presentation, he asked his wife what she thought of the speech.

"Boring, for sure," she replied.

"What about the so-called seven secrets?" he asked. "Did any of them resonate with you?"

She paused. "To tell you the truth, I can't remember any of them. Can you?"

My friend remembered three – which is exactly what I would have expected, and what every effective speaker knows. That's because when it comes to the messages in a spoken presentation, three is *truly* the magic number. Not seven … not five … *three.*

People can easily keep track of and remember things in threes: three ideas, three examples, three milestones, and so forth. In fact, we humans love to group things in threes and we seem to learn things best that way: red, white, and blue … faith, hope, and charity … readin', writin', and 'rithmetic … and all the rest.

Three is also dramatic. It's no accident that classic dramatic structure, as common in TV sitcoms as it is in opera, is based on the three-act format. Act One establishes the characters and situation; in Act Two the situation becomes more complicated and the tension builds; in Act Three the situation is resolved and the tension is released. In fact, every good story has three parts – beginning, middle, end – and so do most good speeches.

Dramatic, engaging, and memorable, the magic of three works in politics, in strategic planning, in describing product features and benefits. And it works like gangbusters in speeches and presentations – both as an overall structural design and as the true magic number for your key messages.

So your next step in the message development process is to get to three – three messages that will bring your audience to understand what you want them to understand, believe what you want them to believe, do what you want them to do. (Notice the three-based structure of that formulation and many others in *It's Showtime!* – I try to practice what I preach.)

Begin by listing your seven or more messages on a white board or piece of paper. Next, make an effort to bundle or categorize the messages on your list. Consider each one, asking yourself what, if anything, it has in common with others. Can you combine any of your messages? Can you bundle two or more into a higher-level category? Are some of them secondary to others – as premises, proof points, reasons why or implications of? If so, set them aside to use later, when you'll be filling out the substance of your presentation.

Keep combining and bundling your messages until you reduce the number to three main messages that will serve as the basis of your presentation.

To return to the example of the health food company executive, she distilled her laundry list of messages to these three:

1. We need to refocus on our core strength: customer service.
2. We need to measure and reward ourselves based on our success.
3. We need to redefine our roles and responsibilities according to a model of "disciplined entrepreneurship."

Your Message Mantra

When you've reduced your laundry list to three essential messages, you have the basis for a presentation that your audience will be able to engage with, care about, keep track of, and – most important of all – *remember* when they go on their merry way.

Or will they?

In our high-speed, media-rich, and message-saturated culture, you simply can't count on your audience to have the patience or the capacity to remember more than one message from your presentation. You have to decide what that one message is, and make it your *message mantra*.

Your message mantra is your macro message – the one message you want your audience to walk away with. It's the single idea, belief, proposal, or call to action that you'll emphasize, repeat, recast, reinvigorate, and hammer home relentlessly, over and over.

Think of someone leaving your presentation and being asked, "What did she say?" Your message mantra is the answer to that question. Another approach: I've worked with PR people who defined their message mantra by asking the question "What is the headline we want to see in print tomorrow?"

Don't be afraid of a message mantra that seems "artsy" or poetic. Many message mantras are metaphors at heart or become metaphors in the course of a presentation.

For example, the health food company president came up with "Go for the sweet spot" as the message mantra for her presentation to employees. She started with an idiom from sports that's become part of the language of business, "the sweet spot." She used it to describe her company's traditional core strength. Then she extended the metaphor to the company's growth opportunities … to customer service as the area where the company must improve and excel … and finally to her idea of "disciplined entrepreneurship."

By the end of her presentation, "Go for the sweet spot" wove together her three key messages. It reminded her audience of the strengths and values that bound them together, it articulated her plan for their future success together, and it described a method for executing that plan. Like Martin Luther King, Jr's "I have a dream," it also became a rallying cry – the ultimate achievement for a message mantra.

When developing the fundraising speech for the president of the religious studies consortium (an example introduced in Chapter 4), the speechwriter found a vivid, powerful message mantra in a story the client and his staff told during our briefing session. The story concerned a philanthropist who wanted to help people affected by the Indian Ocean tsunami of December 2004; in the words of the speech –

> He wanted to help restore the fisheries in the coastal villages of Sumatra. So he offered a *million dollars* to put the boats back in the water. And the aid organization he offered the money to – they turned him down.

> Because, you see, he's Jewish – and the tsunami victims of Sumatra were mostly Muslims.

Opening with this story of a derailed effort to relieve human suffering, the speech established "putting the boats back in the water" as a symbol of what's at stake in building understanding and acceptance among diverse religious faiths. The mantra was invoked again in relation to the failures of public institutions to promote dialogue, tolerance, and healing:

> In the face of so much to discuss and decide, our public discourse is failing us. The rhetoric of oversimplification has taken the place of thoughtful analysis, reasoned argument, and open dialogue … And the politics of polarization carry the day.

> But that kind of rhetoric, that brand of politics doesn't resolve any disagreements or solve any problems. It doesn't move the ball forward – to say nothing of the human race. It doesn't put any boats back in the water.

Finally, in an inspirational call to action, the mantra stood forth as a powerful metaphor for the consortium's core mission and served as a dignified way of doing the essential work of the speech, what all non-profit institutions have to do – ask for money:

> We believe it's not just *possible* to achieve understanding among people of different religions. If humankind is to have a peaceful future, perhaps any future at all, it is imperative that we achieve such understanding.
>
> We are committed to putting the boats back in the water, and we believe it can be done. We ask you to lend a hand.

In the entire speech, "putting the boats back in the water" appeared only three times – four if you take into account that it was also the title of the speech. But that was enough to unite the speech's key messages in a poignant, urgent, and memorable call to action.

A Note on Intentional Redundancy

"Go for the sweet spot! … Go for the sweet spot! … Go for the sweet spot!"

The health food company president was relentless in repeating her message mantra, and her redundancy was entirely intentional. Many presenters worry that they'll appear to be talking down to their audience if they repeat a message mantra too often. They fear that they'll sound like a cheesy late-night TV commercial and lose credibility. On the contrary …

Remember, the ideas and information you deliver may be numbingly familiar to you (indeed, if you've done your homework in developing and rehearsing your presentation, its contents *should* be plenty familiar to you). But in most cases, what you say in your presentation will be entirely new to your audience. They will both need and appreciate the redundancy of an oft-repeated message mantra. Sure, some people will "get it" sooner than others. But they'll be more likely to congratulate themselves for being ahead of the pack than to blame you for making your point abundantly clear.

Keep in mind, too, that your message mantra is not *the whole* of what you have to say. Rather, it's the anchor for everything else, the Rosetta stone your audience will use to understand and synthesize your presentation as they're listening to it and to remember it later.

Finally, as shown in the examples I've described, your message mantra is an anchor for you as well as your audience. By connecting your mantra with the major issues, ideas, and themes covered in your presentation, you'll ensure that your presentation holds together. In other words, your message mantra can serve you in structuring, organizing, and unifying your presentation – tasks discussed in Chapter 8.

Chapter 6
Powerbites

If your English classes were anything like mine, no doubt you learned the basic, tried-and-true techniques of expository writing. You learned to *build* an argument: to announce your thesis ...elaborate and fortify it by marshalling the facts, developing your ideas, and considering and refuting opposing points of view ... and deliver a conclusion that recaps the thesis to a reader now wholly enlightened and convinced. Done right, this kind of exposition is powerful indeed. Like a geometric proof, it proceeds deliberately through a series of logical operations to lay out a solid, coherent, defensible position.

This method still reigns in science and law, where the standards of proof are of the highest order because the stakes are. But in most other walks of life and channels of communication, the leisure to build an argument is a luxury rarely enjoyed by anyone anymore. The world lives on Internet time now. As a professional communicator you can bet that the people in your audience, accustomed to clicking and flicking instantly to what *they* want to read or watch or know *right now,* will want to hear your conclusion sooner rather than later.

That's why I recommend a messaging technique I call the *powerbite.* You're probably familiar with what sales and marketing people speak of as the "elevator pitch" – a descriptive and/or promotional spiel that's brief enough to deliver during an elevator ride. The powerbite is a pitch you can deliver between the first and fifth floors.

Think of the powerbite as a hammer – an aggressive, no-fooling-around tool for driving your message home with a few sharp, precisely-aimed blows. The powerbite responds to the part of your listener's mind that demands, "Prove it – and make it snappy."

How to Build a Powerbite

The powerbite turns the traditional approach to exposition and argument on its head. It *starts* with the conclusion, advances two or three pieces of evidence for that conclusion, and then tells the audience what it means *to them* – all in concise, forceful, vivid language.

Here's the basic recipe for building a powerbite:

1. Begin by asserting your "conclusion." Try to limit this statement to *one sentence.*
2. Next, formulate the evidence for your assertion. You can use facts, data points, or anecdotal stories, but don't use more than three pieces of evidence.
3. Finish by telling your audience what it all means *to them*. This is the payoff, the answer to your listeners' unspoken "So what?"
4. Read through the powerbite out loud – that is, rehearse it – and then go back and revise it as necessary to sharpen the language and heighten the impact.
5. Repeat step 4, and then repeat it again, and again, and …

Now, a few notes on each component of the powerbite:

The opening assertion (your "conclusion"). It's no simple task to start with your conclusion. As rational, logical beings, we're used to working up to a conclusion, and we often learn what it is by thinking through the entire message. For this reason, it may take a good bit of time and effort to formulate your conclusion. And for the same reason, it's always a good idea to go back and revise and sharpen your opening assertion after you've finished drafting the complete powerbite.

The evidence. Why a maximum of three pieces of evidence? As any experienced salesman will tell you, never sell beyond the close – all you do is risk losing the sale. There's no point piling on the proof, hoping to persuade your audience with the sheer weight of it, when all it will really do is confuse them.

How elaborate – and lengthy – should your evidence be? That depends on where, when, and how you're using a powerbite. For example, when using a powerbite as the proverbial elevator pitch or as the answer to a question, conciseness counts, and it's best to keep your evidence short and sweet. When you "have the floor" for a longer time or you face an openly skeptical audience, you're justified in presenting a more elaborate, detailed set of proof points.

The payoff. Ideally, the payoff should be of a more personal nature than the assertion you started with. Remember, it's primarily about your audience – not you, your product, your strategy, or whatever. But the payoff should also be direct and concise. One of its functions is to wrap up your powerbite – or, if I may put it more bluntly, to get you to stop talking.

Dressing Up Your Powerbites

In powerbites every word counts, and the richer, more vivid, more *specific* the language you use, the more powerful your powerbites will be. Having heard more than one executive let the air out of a presentation by using *amazing* over and over, I've compiled the following list of adjectives that can be substituted for that tired old term. You can probably add your own to the list. And I recommend that you compile your own list of forceful, energetic words for dressing up your powerbites.

unique	electric	inspired
matchless	exciting	immense
extraordinary	confident	vast
rare	jazzed	infinite
distinctive	stoked	ingenious
one-of-a-kind	energized	creative
singular	hopeful	huge
incomparable	eager	original
exceptional	thrilled	limitless
astonishing	powerful	eye-popping
remarkable	intense	rich
startling	deep	far-reaching
surprising	extreme	astounding
mind-blowing	dynamic	gripping
passionate	dazzling	brilliant
jaw-dropping	potent	breathtaking
fun	competitive	majestic
robust	fierce	grand

How to Use Powerbites

Powerbites are extraordinarily versatile. You can use them in all kinds of ways and contexts and for all kinds of purposes. That's why I urge virtually all of my clients to develop a set of powerbites for all of their important communications challenges.

A powerbite can function as your "hook" for a visitor to your place of business or tradeshow booth. It can serve as a way of introducing yourself to someone you meet at a conference or a cocktail party. As your contributions to a conference or panel discussion, powerbites will help audience members quickly grasp and long remember your message. Along with the moderator and your fellow speakers, the audience will also appreciate your brevity, in contrast to the windbag who hogs the microphone without saying anything.

A single powerbite can become the blueprint for an entire speech. As components of a speech, powerbites can serve as a direct, dramatic opening; as a "to-summarize-so-far" signpost in the body of the speech; and as a high-impact, memorable conclusion. You can build longer messages, even whole speeches, from powerbites. One technique for doing this is what I call *cascading powerbites*. You start with one powerbite, then follow it with powerbites based on each piece of evidence it included, and so on. (I've included an example of cascading powerbites at the end of this chapter.)

I believe powerbites are *the most effective way* of answering questions, and not only questions from journalists and financial analysts. Most of us are asked the same questions over and over in our business and professional lives (and our personal lives, too, I suppose). What do you do? Why should I buy your product? Why are we making this change? Is this the best strategy? Powerbites can simplify your life by enabling you to answer such recurring questions without having to compose a new response each time. They can also enable you to give your best answer every time – one that you've thought through, created, and rehearsed for maximum impact.

One of the greatest gifts you can give yourself as a communicator is a supply of carefully crafted powerbites for all of the communications challenges you face: product launches, management and employee meetings, strategic and organizational initiatives, press conferences, analyst briefings, performance reviews, career changes, you name it. Accessing the power of persuasion is a matter of being prepared. With powerbites, you are.

Keep in mind that powerbites come in different sizes. As I've noted when discussing the use of evidence, in some contexts you'll make a powerbite most powerful by making it brief. In other contexts, you can give a powerbite more scope. You can enrich the language, use more detail, and relate longer anecdotes as evidence. (In the next chapter, I address the importance of stories in persuasive communications.) I recommend that you create both short and long versions of your powerbites, to use as the occasion demands.

Finally, remember that every act of communication must be tailored for the audience. In a legal firm, for example, a powerbite designed for potential clients will require some modification before you can use it with a recruit or a new hire. In healthcare, you might use the same basic powerbites to deliver key messages to patients, vendors, and regulators – but because those different audiences "speak different languages," you'd want to recast your powerbites for each one. Powerbites built for a product launch can be used to address customers, the channel, the analyst community, and others – but you'll need to adjust the language, tone, and emphasis for each group. So as you develop your arsenal of powerbites, make sure that you create variations that are appropriate for the various audiences you'll face.

Sample Powerbites

I answer the question "What do you do?":

Conclusion	I help people make high-stakes, highly successful presentations in their own style.
Evidence	I help leaders at technology companies like Microsoft, Infospace, and ATI launch new products and speak to analysts, the financial community, and the press.
Evidence	I help leaders of companies like Schwab, ClifBar, ADP, and VISA speak to customers and drive culture change within their companies.
Evidence	I help lawyers at firms like Sidley Austin and Liebert Cassidy Whitmore develop client relationships, prepare witnesses, and win in the courtroom.
So what?	I can help you succeed in your next presentation and in all your business and professional communications.

I "reduce the sauce" to answer the same question more succinctly:

Conclusion	I help people make high-stakes, highly successful presentations.
Evidence	I help CEOs talk to the press.
Evidence	I help lawyers win in the courtroom.
Evidence	I help leaders lead through effective communications.
So what?	I can help you with your presentations.

A legal firm speaks to potential clients:

Conclusion	LCW is the only place to turn for your labor and employment counsel.
Evidence	Our team approach puts world-class experience on your side, whatever the issue (insert selective bios of partners or "walk down the hall" anecdote of collaboration among partners).
Evidence	Our aggressive prevention education will lower your risk of litigation (describe workshops).
Evidence	If you do need to take an issue to court, we have the experience and know-how to provide the best advocacy (provide an example or data).

So what?	Expert legal counsel could make the crucial difference in your company's success and/or your career – that's why LCW is your only choice.

A technology company tells consumers about a new product:

Conclusion	The Smartphone delivers the future of cell phone communications now.
Evidence	It's a great phone with easy navigation and access to all your contacts.
Evidence	It's your on-the-go connection to your e-mail and the entire World Wide Web.
Evidence	It allows you to enjoy your digital media – music, movies, and photos – anywhere.
So what?	When it's time for your next cell phone – or your next cell phone call – make it the Smartphone.

A healthcare enterprise tells doctors why they should join:

Conclusion	Kaiser Permanente's healthcare model gives us a clear competitive advantage, enabling us to outperform other healthcare models during these turbulent times.
Evidence	Our quality of care is incomparable, as more and more people are recognizing (insert data).
Evidence	Our recent service improvements have been far-reaching (insert data) and validate our superior strategic approach.
Evidence	Our integrated model continues to produce dynamic economies and efficiencies along with an unrivaled quality of outcomes (insert example).
So what?	As a KP doctor, your future is secure.

The same enterprise "reduces the sauce":

Conclusion	Kaiser Permanente has a clear competitive advantage.
Evidence	Our quality of care is superior (insert data).
Evidence	Our service improvements are significant (insert customer satisfaction data).
Evidence	Our integrated model continues to produce superior economies and efficiencies (insert example).
So what?	As a KP doctor, you work with the best medical group in the country.

A technology company tells consumers about a new product:

Conclusion	The next generation of videogame entertainment begins now with Xbox 360, the most powerful entertainment platform on the planet.
Evidence	Xbox 360 puts you at the center of great games like (list two or three key game titles).
Evidence	Xbox 360 connects you to gamers like you around the world for competition and community (show new UI and Xbox Live features).
Evidence	It's all the best of digital entertainment, not just video games (play a DVD and/or plug in the music player and play music).
So what?	Xbox 360 will change the way you think about fun.

The same company builds the first of several cascading powerbites, starting with the first piece of evidence from the basic powerbite above as the conclusion of this one:

Conclusion	Xbox 360 puts you at the center of great games like (list two or three key game titles).
Evidence	It renders your games in high-definition graphics (show HD graphics)
Evidence	Xbox 360 gives you sound such as you've never heard it (turn up the sound).
Evidence	Xbox 360 games explode with great stories and rich characters (show new game).
So what?	Xbox 360 will satisfy your passion for spectacular, state-of-the-art videogame entertainment.

The same company adapts the payoff of its basic powerbite for various audiences:

For consumers (original):

So what?	Xbox 360 will change the way you think about fun.

For retailers:

So what?	Xbox 360 is the must-have entertainment product for everyone this holiday season.

For financial analysts:

So what?	Xbox 360 will lead the way in creating a market of half a billion gamers in the next ten years.

For industry analysts:

    So what?   Xbox 360 establishes Microsoft's market leadership in the next generation of games and entertainment.

For technology analysts:

    So what?   The Xbox 360 platform confirms that a combination of hardware, software, and services will drive the future of digital entertainment.

Exercise:

Building a Powerbite

Use this template to create two powerbites to answer the question, "What do you do?" First, compose a 90-second version; then "reduce the sauce" to craft a version you can deliver in 20 or 30 seconds.

Conclusion

Evidence

Evidence

Evidence

So what?

Exercise:

Powerbite Answers for Various Audiences

Use this worksheet to articulate answers to the most pressing questions facing you and your organization (modify as needed). Then, using the template provided in the previous exercise, build powerbite answers to each question. Finally, customize each powerbite for the various audiences specified.

Question 1:   Why is _____ critical to our continued success?

Audiences: Internal, external

Question 2 :   Why is it important to pursue _____ strategy?

Audiences: Your manager or leader, your direct reports

Question 3:   Why is the investment in _____ critical to our continued success?

Audiences: The CEO of your organization, the CFO, the board of directors

Question 4:   What is the value to our customers of offering
               _____?
Audiences: Customers, retailers/channel partners, board of directors

Question 5:   What is compelling and different about our offer?
Audiences: All

Question 6:   Why should we participate in _____
               organizational initiative? (training, realignment, etc.)
Audience: Your organization, your manager, your direct reports

Question 7:   Why is this company poised for success?
Audiences: Your team, your customers

Chapter 7
Storytelling

*We need story; otherwise the tremendous randomness
of experience overwhelms us. Story is what penetrates.*
— Robert Coover

Everyone loves a good story.

The need for story runs deep in our species. Cultures define themselves through stories called myths. Religions embody their values and beliefs in stories. Nations rely on stories – the Trojan War, the six wives of Henry the Eighth, the Great Depression – to conceptualize, understand, and pass down their histories from generation to generation. Parents tell stories to teach their children. Stories are what we use to try to make sense of the world and ourselves. As the philosopher Kenneth Burke said, "Stories are equipment for living."

We learn to talk and listen by having people read stories to us, and we learn to read by parsing their words and sentences for ourselves. Story is the very essence of our narrative and dramatic arts, from epic poetry and the novel to theater, film, and television. Even the news of the day is packaged in the form of stories.

Why are stories so powerful, so important, so central to our lives?

To begin with, stories are mostly about *people*. We are a gossipy tribe. From the back fence to Broadway, the campfire to the cineplex, we never tire of telling and hearing stories, about ourselves and about others. Stories give us a way to compare notes about being human. Stories present us with actions we have done or can imagine doing, experiences we have had or can imagine having.

More: Stories are about feelings – in contrast to the proofs of logic or appeals to reason, which speak to the brain, stories speak to the heart. Stories go to our core.

Stories are dramatic. Whether played out by actors, read from the page, shared around a kitchen or conference room table, or told from a podium, great stories command our attention with that irresistible question: What will happen next? They can draw us to the edge of our seats – literally – in anticipation of the answer, and they can take our breath away when they deliver it.

Finally, and most important in the context of this book, stories are *persuasive*. Don't get me wrong. Stories told purely to entertain have value, and I've watched many speakers use such stories to make themselves and the occasion memorable, which can only enhance the impact of a presentation.

That said, the great power and purpose of stories in business and professional communications is to make a point. You can claim that your product or service is superior; but you can prove it with a story. You can spell out your company's principles or cultural values; but you can illustrate them and validate them with stories. You can describe what "differentiates" your brand; but you can make your brand both unmistakable and unforgettable with stories. You can suggest that people act or change, or even ask them directly; but you can jolt them into action or inspire them to change with a story.

Storytelling Types and Examples

In my experience, six types of stories are most common – and, I believe, most effective – in business and professional presentations:

- The Anecdote
- The Powerbite Story
- The Hero Story
- The Cautionary Tale
- The Aspirational Story
- The Analogy

Of course, many stories are a combination of two or more of these types. But let's consider the six basic types before turning our attention to the techniques of effective storytelling.

The Anecdote. The Greek root of the word *anecdote* means "unpublished items," and indeed anecdotes are usually just that: brief narratives of events that never made the six o'clock news or the *New York Times*. People sometimes speak of "anecdotal evidence" dubiously if not with scorn. But in a presentation, anecdotes can often serve to prove a point more effectively than a dry set of facts.

Here's an anecdote used by one of my clients in the healthcare industry:

Dr. Avila recently experienced a moment all doctors fear. He made
a medical error during a routine colonoscopy. Thank goodness the

error was detected early, and a potentially life-threatening infection was avoided. But in the meantime, the patient and her husband were extremely anxious and very angry.

There was no question that a mistake had been made and a lawsuit was a very real possibility. In the past, Dr. Avila would have avoided further contact with the patient and her family, lest anything he might say would further expose his liability. But he had recently completed our training program in risk management, where he learned that a provider can express concern and sorrow in such a situation – that, in fact, he *should* express concern and sorrow – without incurring greater liability.

As a result, Dr. Avila was able to sit down with the patient and her husband and express his sincere regret that the event had taken place. He explained what had happened during the procedure, then talked about steps he was already taking to make sure that such an error would not happen again. Human and heartfelt, his honesty served as a first step in mending the provider-patient relationship and, ultimately, helped us avoid a costly lawsuit. During their exit briefing, the patient and her husband expressed their appreciation for Dr. Avila and stated that from their point of view the case was closed.

This is just one example of how honest, whole-hearted communication with patients can reduce our exposure to lawsuits. Now let me show you some statistics that prove how the training and skills Dr. Avila brought to bear on his case are having a positive impact on risk across our organization.

Notice how the speaker first told a story to dramatize and humanize the issues, then turned to the statistics showing that risk management training benefits everyone in the organization, not just the individual featured in the story. This is the power of the anecdote, to engage an audience in a particular case as a means of driving home a broader point.

Here's another example of an anecdote that was used in a fundraising speech for a religious studies consortium (also discussed in Chapter 5):

The day after Christmas last year, we learned that an earthquake-triggered tsunami had struck coastal areas surrounding the Indian Ocean.

It was a faraway disaster — literally on the other side of the world — and at first our media tried to "bring it home" to us with stories of Western tourists who were there, caught in the wrong place at the wrong time.

But as the death toll mounted, it became clear that the story was not about Western tourists. On the westernmost Indonesian island of Sumatra, which was closest to the epicenter and already in turmoil because of civil war, more than 100,000 people had died. Half a million were left homeless.

And in villages along the coast, the tsunami had also destroyed the fishing industry, which the people there depend on for food, for trade, for life itself.

A death toll over 150,000, and a human toll that staggered the imagination — that's what brought the story home to concerned people everywhere.

One such person — a man I know because he happens to be one of our donors — this man felt called upon to do something in the wake of that faraway disaster. He wanted to help restore the fisheries in the coastal villages of Sumatra. So he offered a million dollars to put the boats back in the water. And the aid organization he offered the money to — they turned him down.

Because, you see, he's Jewish — and the tsunami victims of Sumatra were mostly Muslims.

Isn't that typical of the world today? Just one more irony in our sad, ironic times?

I hope not. I hope we're still capable of understanding such episodes as *tragic* — all the more so because we've come to think of them as *typical*.

Notice how the greater part of the story was given over to exposition; the Indian Ocean tsunami of late 2004 is what set up the drama of the story — what was at stake — so the speaker took his time establishing and letting the audience connect with that background. Then, at the end, the speaker drove home the point of the anecdote in a distinctive way: first he offered himself and the audience a chance to distance themselves from the outcome as "just one more irony," and then he forcefully withdrew that option.

The Powerbite Story. Simply put, this is a series of anecdotes strung together as the evidence in a powerbite. Instead of data, facts, or assertions, you use an exemplary or illustrative anecdote for each piece of evidence.

For example, here's a powerbite about a legal firm that specializes in labor and employment issues (used as an example in Chapter 6):

Conclusion	LCW is the only place to turn for your labor and employment counsel.
Evidence	Our aggressive preventative education will lower your risk of litigation.
Evidence	Our team approach puts world-class experience at your command.
Evidence	If you do need to take an issue to court, we have the experience and know-how to provide you with the best advocacy.

So what? Because expert legal counsel could make the difference in your company's success and your career, LCW is your best choice.

And here's a "translation" of that powerbite into the story of a city manager whose career is enhanced by use of effective counsel:

"Peggy Gets Promoted"

A Valentine City administrator named Peggy Whitman is just one of the many clients we serve here at LCW. She's been attending our workshops in conflict resolution, discipline, evaluations, and more for the last six years, and as she'll be the first to tell you, that training has helped her in countless ways. For example, she's developed a "don't wait" approach to employee feedback and performance evaluation. Not only did this help her justify the reassigning of an underperforming staff member; it also improved overall morale among her team.

But Peggy's most compelling success at the city involved the restructuring of her department to better serve the community. At one point, three of our partners joined forces to help her navigate the most complex aspects of the personnel changes. Peggy loves to tell the story of the conference call she had with two additional partners, during which one rattled off FLSA requirements while the other offered tips and learnings from a similar process we had just helped a client with.

In court, we were pleased to represent Peggy and the city and prevail in a case that helped set a precedent for cities trying to improve their services to the community.

And we are proud to say that Peggy Whitman has recently been promoted by the city of Valentine – a promotion she richly deserves.

Notice how the story follows the structure of the powerbite, with an incident or detail serving to document each piece of evidence and to answer the question "So what?"

The Hero Story. Heroes are people who make a difference, which makes them very useful in speeches and presentations where *you* want to make a difference. But what makes heroes heroic – and what makes their stories dramatic and compelling – is that they must overcome obstacles in order to succeed. Joan of Arc started out as the daughter of peasants, not as a priest or courtier or soldier; Horatio Alger was decidedly *not* born with a silver spoon in his mouth; Luke Skywalker didn't know that he *could be* a Jedi knight, much less how.

The scholar of mythology Joseph Campbell taught us to think of the hero's struggle as a journey, whether real or metaphorical. This can serve as a useful guideline when you're creating your own hero stories. Think of yourself as narrating a journey. Where does your hero set out from? What obstacles arise along the way, and how is each one overcome? What is the decisive moment in the story, sometimes called the moment of resolution, when the hero overcomes the last obstacle, arrives at his or her destination, learns or understands something new, or makes a crucial decision? In short, what happens to *change* the hero, or when the hero *changes* the world?

This story, used in the fundraising speech for the religious studies consortium, makes powerful, dramatic use of the decisive moment in the hero's journey:

Amazing people find their way to us in amazing ways. And they arrive with a sense of mission that's rooted in their faith but energized by their experience in the world. It's their passion, their engagement, that makes the GTU a place where religion meets the world.

One of my favorite examples is Elizabeth Drescher, a doctoral student in Christian spirituality. Before coming to the GTU, Elizabeth worked for some years in health insurance. During that time she discovered what she believed to be improper procedures that had defrauded the government and denied benefits to thousands of people. Convinced that her employer had no intention of correcting the problem, she reported it to the government.

But it's one thing to become a whistleblower, quite another to undertake doctoral studies in theology at the GTU. What brought Elizabeth to us? Here are her own words on the connection:

> My work at the GTU is aimed at understanding why people do or do not feel empowered to act upon their religious commitments. For instance, what moved in the soul of the woman who put a pile of Medicare reports on my chair with a note saying, "I have been trying for years to get this fixed, but have been told that I'd be fired if I brought it up again. I have two small children and cannot lose my job. I've heard that you're working on this … I hope this will help you." And, she added, "I am praying for you."

It probably won't surprise you that Elizabeth's doctoral research is focused on what she calls "the faith lives of ordinary Christians." Or that she is passionate about the connection between her research and current issues, like the role of religion in contemporary American politics.

It's not surprising that this story was at the heart of a speech about the values and mission of an organization. It's also interesting that it was, in fact, a story within a story: a tale of one person with certain values inspiring another, and that person in turn embodying those values for someone else (in this case, for the speaker as well as for the audience). Hero stories are especially good for communicating the core values of an organization and propagating those values through the organization and beyond.

A little less poetic, perhaps, but equally effective is the hero story in which a product, service, or system, rather than a person, is the hero. For example, a client of mine named Dr. David Lawrence opened a speech before the National Press Club with the story of a 15-year-old asthma sufferer named Maria and her family. A mesmerizing storyteller, Dr. Lawrence described the trials and tribulations they went through to get Maria the care she needed in a fee-for-service medical system: the trips to the emergency room … the "near misses" when inappropriate medications were almost administered … even the disappointment of Maria's little brother that family vacation trips were out of the question because his sister could not stray from the one medical center the family could visit.

Enter the hero, as Maria and her family are able to access team-based care provided by an integrated healthcare organization. The whole story changes, as the team teaches Maria and her parents better methods for controlling and treating her asthma. Her electronic medical record, including all of her prescriptions, is available to providers anywhere in the state. At the end we see the family – and a happy little brother – going on their first vacation in years because Maria's health is improved and she can count on exceptional care along the entire route.

Though it featured a non-human hero – integrated, team-based healthcare – Dr. Lawrence's story was nevertheless rich in human interest, action, and drama. Stories in which technology is the hero, increasingly common in our ever-more-digital world, can be just as effective. For example, a client who built a successful company selling bar coding technology to hospitals told this story:

> Every year thousands of patients die due to medical errors in the administration of prescriptions. And no wonder! Consider Mrs. Crosby, a woman in her seventies who arrived at the hospital for surgery with seven bottles of prescription drugs in a paper bag. Now the effects of her surgery have left her even less clear than she already was about which of those to take and when. The nurse on duty is overworked and tired, and the physician who prescribed Mrs. Crosby's additional post-op meds did so in his usual illegible scribble. And to top it all off, many of the medication containers, old and new, look alike.
>
> A recipe for disaster? Of course it was – *until* Fairmont Hospital rolled out a simple bar code system that requires staff to scan *any* medication before it's given to a patient. Now Mrs. Crosby's prescriptions are entered into the system when she arrives. The physician's instructions are entered, too – and accurately deciphered in the process. And no matter how tired and distracted he or she might be, no nurse will be able to administer a medication until the system confirms that it's the right medication at the right dose.

The Cautionary Tale. "Train wrecks" are irresistible spectacles. Who doesn't like a woeful tale of failure, heartbreak, or horror? The patient who got "back-watered" in the emergency room and nearly died. The potentially ruinous liability lawsuit brought about by a perfect storm of product failure and organizational dysfunction. The price that had to be paid when a company went too long without paying attention to customers.

Here's one such story an executive used in a presentation to the employees of his company.

Last quarter our sales team sold applications to fifty new customers, and we promised they'd be up and running within three months. But because they had bought multiple applications, these customers started getting calls from several of our implementation teams, who all asked them the same questions and asked them to fill out the same forms.

Naturally, the customers started to complain. But our sales team didn't get the head's-up, and they had no way of knowing that their sweet success of the recent past was quickly turning sour.

That wasn't all. As you know, our products are not integrated, the interface for each is different, and so users need different training for each application. Apparently, our training teams don't communicate with one another any better than our implementation and sales teams. So we had two or three trainers calling customers and clamoring to train them – at the same time.

Is it any wonder that our fail-to-start rate with these customers is at 68 percent?

This example illustrates both the power and the perils of the cautionary tale. There can be no question what the moral of this story is – that rhetorical question at the end is like a twist of the knife. But what a downer!

Two words of warning about cautionary tales …

First, I believe the cautionary tale is overused these days. Seduced by the doomsday drama of it all, too many speakers are opting for what's called a "burning platform" presentation, presumably in an effort to jolt the audience into action. Some of these presentations feature a tale of abject failure like the one above. In others, a single slide showing an unsustainable trend does the job of painting a bleak picture. But unbeknownst to these speakers of doom and gloom, many are delivering the fifth "burning platform" presentation the audience has had to listen to in the last week. Bad enough that you come off sounding like Chicken Little ("The sky is falling!"); you definitely don't want to be one of many such downcast, panicky creatures.

Second, when you tell a cautionary tale, you are taking a risk: that a feeling of being blamed (and fearing the consequences) might overwhelm your audience, or that failure will be the only thing they'll remember from your presentation. Dishearten an audience too much and you can alienate them and never get them back; they will literally tune you out for the rest of your presentation.

So I advise caution when using cautionary tales. In any case, avoid *starting* a presentation with a cautionary tale – that is, before you've had a chance to establish rapport and trust with the audience. And *always* balance a cautionary tale with something positive and upbeat: a "what we learned" plan for saving the day or doing better next time, a tale of turning the tide, a happy ending or aspirational story that restores the audience's sense of hope.

The Aspirational Story. I believe that aspirational storytelling, introduced in the context of vision in Chapter 3, is one of the most powerful techniques available to business and professional communicators. A form of storytelling that some people call *future-casting,* the aspirational story actually takes place in the future, creating a picture of what that future will look and feel like.

In an aspirational story, you can describe the change, results, innovations, systems, or values you wish to bring about. That's why this form of storytelling is so useful for leaders at every level: by giving specific, detailed, compelling form to your vision, you can transform your *aspirations* into *inspiration* for those you lead or work with. You can motivate people to do great things.

Perhaps because it's completely "made up" – a tale of things that have not yet come to pass – the aspirational story gives full scope to the art of storytelling. You can describe a day in the life of an organization or team, a customer or a client. You can take the audience on an experiential journey, building in moments when a new system or product is enjoyed, a task is made simpler than ever before, something perhaps not even imagined becomes something real.

Here's an example. A manager at Genentech stands before her team of 250 employees. She has mocked up a copy of *The Wall Street Journal* and displays it to the audience.

> I'd like to read you a front-page article from *The Wall Street Journal* of May 15th, 2012, under the headline "Genentech: Delivering Cures for Both Patients and Investors."
>
> The article begins like this: "With the release of its latest cancer drug, biotech pioneer Genentech has proved once again the power of genetics-based drug development to help patients seeking a cure for deadly disease as well as investors looking for healthy returns."
>
> The story jumps to page four, where it's accompanied by a sidebar under this headline: "Data Delivery Accelerates Approval Process." That's right, folks: that's our organization, right here in a front-page

story in the *Journal.* According to the article, *we* made the crucial difference in ensuring rapid FDA approval. *We* are credited with getting the right information to the right people on a timely basis throughout the clinical trials and approval process. *Our* analytics are described as, quote, *second to none in the industry,* unquote.

And what started the journey to this triumphant day in the year 2012? It started when we met as a team on this day in 2007 and committed to three key objectives that gave us focus, drove our decisions, and inspired our excellence in the years to come.

This leader uses the aspirational story as a hook to introduce her strategic priorities. To be sure, both she and her audience know that these priorities will require hard work and change. She is counting on the aspirational story to motivate that change.

The analogy. As the playwright Christopher Fry wrote, "What a wonderful thing is metaphor!" By using one thing to describe another, analogies actually help people see things differently and often, therefore, more clearly – in a new light, so to speak.

Analogies can be long or short. In his book *Raising the Bar: Integrity and Passion in Life and Business,* outdoor adventurer and Clif Bar founder Gary Erickson tells a story (originally used in a presentation) of a failed climb up an icy mountain face as an analogy for a period when his company lost its focus, adaptability, and initiative. Another leader I worked with used a brief analogy we can all relate to – the panic of trying to find the windshield wipers in a rental car when a sudden downpour rendered him virtually blind at 60 miles per hour – to highlight why a common user interface is essential to the future of his industry.

Often known as a *parable,* the analogy has a long and honorable history in religion and myth. The following story, used by a data processing executive in his keynote address at a client conference, draws on scripture for an analogy.

Let me begin with a very old story: the story of the Tower of Babel, from the *Bible's* Book of Genesis.

As you may remember, this is a story about Noah's descendents. The first thing we're told about them – and this is very important – is that they shared a common language. The next thing we know, they settle in Babylon, and they decide to build a tower that reaches up to heaven. It's their way of making a name for themselves.

But God sees this tower, and he – or she – doesn't like it one bit. Too presumptuous. If mankind succeeds with this, who knows what they'll try next, right? So God takes away their common language, and scatters them in confusion. And that puts an end to work on the tower. After all, it's tough to build a tower to heaven when you can't understand what the guy next to you is saying.

I wouldn't be surprised if you've heard this story before, applied to our industry and the way we've been using technology. The Tower of Babel gets lost in the babble. Instead of a common language, we have the confusion and conflict of many systems and tools and applications. There's lots of talk, but not much understanding.

Notice how the speaker recast the story in modern colloquial language, making sure to avoid offending anyone's religious sensibilities while encouraging the audience to see themselves in the story. Notice, too, that the speaker was very explicit in articulating the moral of the story and relating it to the audience.

Time to Revive a "Lost Art"

Given the power of storytelling, I've been surprised to discover how rarely stories are used in today's business and professional presentations. Among my clients, I've found that lawyers are the most likely to recognize the importance of storytelling. Perhaps this is because so much of the law is case law – fundamentally a body of stories. In a certain sense, too, litigation is a form of competitive storytelling, and many of the greatest litigators in history have been superb storytellers.

But among most professionals and business people, it seems, storytelling has become a lost art. (Even litigators, I've observed, lose the knack when conducting the business and management sides of their profession.) Has storytelling fallen victim to the hurry-up pace of the workaday world? When facing audiences who demand facts and figures, logic and proof, are we afraid that they'll regard stories with suspicion – that they'll find our stories artificial, at best ambiguous, at worst frivolous? As we've become dependent on presentation software that's more about the software than the presentation, has storytelling been felled by a hail of bullet points?

Whatever the reasons we may have turned away from it, I'm a ferocious advocate for reviving the lost art of storytelling in business and professional communications. As demonstrated, I hope, by the examples I've described, stories have an unparalleled power to command attention and engage the heart as well as the mind: theirs is the true power of persuasion.

Besides, it's just plain fun to tell and listen to stories. Whether you're the speaker or an audience member, you can count on storytelling to give any presentation an extra charge of vitality.

So what keeps more people from exploiting this potent form of communication? In most cases, I've found, it's fear. You can't imagine how often I hear people marvel at the great stories they hear and the people who tell them – and then claim that they themselves are just no good at telling stories.

I don't buy it. As I started this chapter by saying, we all tell and hear stories all the time. We have a natural affinity for stories and storytelling. And we can all become good storytellers.

How to Learn to Tell a Story

You've probably heard the saying about writing: *Good writers borrow from other writers; great writers steal from them outright.* The same can be said of storytellers. One of the best ways to develop and refine your own storytelling skills is to beg, borrow, and steal from other storytellers.

It starts with listening for good stories – and then *really* listening to them. Instead of simply getting lost in the story, pay attention to its structure and how it's being told. Then, soon after hearing a good story, tell it to someone else. See how well you can replicate the structure, the language, the pacing, the descriptions and details and flourishes that made it so effective when you heard it.

In the meantime, familiarize yourself with the basics of story structure and storytelling technique …

How to Tell a Story: Structure

Storytelling is a narrative form, which is to say that the fundamental axis of a story is time: *"This happened, then this happened, then …."* Of course, a series of simply random events do not a story make; there has to be something that holds the events together in a coherent whole.

The simplest way to describe the structure of a story is that it has a beginning, a middle, and an end. Just as important, to command our attention and hold our interest, what happens in a story must happen to someone. In fact, it is that someone who holds the events together. Every story has a leading character, known in drama as the protagonist, whose actions and experiences engage the audience's interest.

As Aristotle explained in his observations on Greek drama, the most compelling stories reach a turning point in either a *moment of reversal* in the fortunes of the protagonist, or a *moment of recognition* when the protagonist learns something new, or both. In any case, the protagonist is *changed*.

Adding up these observations, we might describe the structure of most stories like this:

1. Something happens to someone …
2. That person and others take action in response to what has happened …
3. And the final result is that change takes place – in the external or internal circumstances of the protagonist.

Adding a little more detail, here's how I'd describe the basic building blocks for a story:

"Once upon a time …" Implicitly, at least, just about all stories begin with the classic fairy tale opening, as the storyteller introduces us to the protagonist and other characters (whom the story is about) and the setting (when and where it takes place). This part of the story is also known as the *exposition.*

"Then one day …" Something happens, and that "something" triggers the rest of the action of the story, usually propelling the protagonist on the path to some goal. In drama and screenwriting, the triggering event is often called the *inciting incident.*

"And then … and then … and then …" The plot thickens, as one action or event after another unfolds. In dramatic writing, these developments are known as *complications* because, well, things get complicated. In well-crafted stories, each complication results from and/or builds on the one before it.

"Until at last …" In drama, this is called the *resolution* or *denouement* – from the French word *desnouer,* "to untie" – as the story's big knot of complications gets untangled. For Aristotle, this is the so-called moment of reversal. In any case, it is the all-important moment of change.

"And the moral of the story is …" This is the end. The cliché about "the moral of the story" is usually reserved for children's stories or, if used in stories told by and for adults, it's used somewhat ironically. But in business and professional presentations, it's important to close a story with the end results, the lessons learned, the benefits reaped ("And because of that …" or "And ever since then …"). Indeed, interpreting or elaborating on the meaning of a story, as described in the next section, can be a very persuasive tactic.

How to Tell a Story: Technique

As a reader or listener, you know that there's more to storytelling than simply saying "what happened." You know that much of the power of a story comes from the art with which it is told. Here are a few basic techniques for making your stories more engaging, more dramatic, more persuasive:

Give every story a title. By starting off a story with a title, you can pique the audience's interest – and give them a way to remember the story later. Even if you don't share it with the audience, giving a title to every story you plan to tell will force you to think about why you're telling it. You'll focus better on the story's theme, essence, or core message – and the story will be the better for it.

Make it dramatic. Without drama, a story is just one thing happening after another. Keeping your eye on the structure of your story can help you make it dramatic. What do you need to reveal during the exposition at the beginning to set up the plot and "seed" the tension? Just as important, what do you need to *conceal*? How many actions and events (complications), told in how much detail, will build the tension without exhausting the patience of the audience? At what point *exactly* should your denouement arrive, and what's the most effective way of delivering it?

Add "color." When you show an audience a PowerPoint presentation or demonstrate a product, they all see the same thing. When you tell them a story, you engage them as collaborators, inviting them to imagine the story in their own minds. That's what makes storytelling so powerful. And that's why it's essential to use language and imagery that makes your story vivid in the "mind's eye" of each listener.

With *descriptive coloring*, you use words to paint a picture of what the characters and settings look like, to tell *how* people behaved and not just *what* they did. Such details add texture and specificity to the characters and events. With *emotional coloring,* you enable your audience to connect and empathize with what the characters feel. Here are some examples of both kinds of coloring –

> He sailed into the room looking like some sort of high-tech rock star.

> Realizing that finger-pointing would be a waste of time, they trudged back to their cubicles and started over.

> You could see the steam coming out of her ears, and you could think of a lot of places you'd rather be.

> The results jolted the industry like a hundred million volts, and back at the office we broke out the champagne.

> The defendant sat stony-faced as the judge read the verdict in silence and handed it back to the bailiff.

Use multiple points of view. A good story becomes great when you approach it from multiple points of view. Take, for example, the story about bar code technology and the difference it can make in a hospital. Told from the point of view of patients, the technology saves lives. Told from the point of view of the nurse, it saves her bacon. Told from the point of view of the physician, it saves a patient and protects a reputation. Told from the point of view of the hospital's risk manager, it saves the hospital from litigation. And told from the point of view of CEO or marketing officer, it differentiates the hospital from others.

Make it sing. Good storytellers have a sense of speech as music – that is, they know how to vary the volume, pitch, and rhythm of their voices to suit each moment in the story. During the exposition, as the characters and situation are introduced, a good storyteller usually goes at a careful and measured pace. As the conflict starts to heat up and tension builds, the pace quickens. And just before the dramatic climax, there's often a "pregnant pause" as the audience waits to hear what will happen next … and the storyteller *makes* them wait. Then, from the climax or resolution to the end of the story, the storyteller often reverts to the relaxed pace of the exposition. In large part, making a story sing is a matter of responding to it emotionally *yourself,* as you tell it. You don't have to be a great actor to do this; with some of the techniques described in Part II for using your voice and body effectively, you can make your stories sing.

Interpret your story. When the purpose of a story is persuasion, as opposed to pure entertainment, interpreting it is often necessary, and always effective, in "closing the deal." Having told the story, you circle back, analyze it, and elaborate on what it means. This is what a leader in healthcare did at the end of a hero story about a doctor saving a child's life –

> The point of this story is not that one individual did something Herculean, something no one else is likely to emulate; on the contrary, the point is that this physician's experience is *not* unique in our organization. We are structured so that *every* physician can have immediate access to a specialist – our governance puts the choice in *your* hands and not those of a bean-counter or utilization review board. Electronically making lab results available to both you and a specialist, even hundreds of miles away, is *standard operating procedure.* So your decision-making can *always* be based on *all* the medical evidence and the most expert consultation. That's why I'm so proud to be part of this organization, and so confident in our ability to provide superior care.

Where's Your Story Room?

Every successful business succeeds by differentiating its products and services, their features and benefits, in the eyes of its customers. Likewise, every enterprise, institution, company, department, group, team, and partnership is built on certain core values that bind all the members together in a shared understanding, a common goal, a united effort.

But it's impossible to differentiate products or the values of your organization using only features, facts, and figures. And it usually doesn't work to simply lay claim to superiority. Saying that your product is faster, more powerful, or "better," that you have integrity, that you're customer-focused or innovative, that you care about your employees or your community – as often as not, such assertions provoke doubt or even derision. "After all," your audience is likely to think, "doesn't everybody say that?" Claims sound empty without something concrete, something the listener connects with, to back them up.

Storytelling is the answer. Brought to life in stories, the key attributes and benefits of your product or service or the core values of your organization become not only credible but vivid, specific, powerful, and memorable.

Maybe yours is simply not a storytelling organization – or so you think. I've found that if you listen, and maybe do a bit of prodding, you can hear many stories, just buzzing with life and lessons, in any organization.

Differentiating products or services through storytelling. I frequently work with clients who are planning a product launch, press tour, or other campaign to introduce their new offerings to the marketplace. One of the most useful exercises we can go through, I've found, is to gather the team in front of a big white board and build what I call a story room.

We begin by populating the board with all the features and benefits we can think of. Usually, the list gets pretty long, at which point it's time to reduce the sauce. When we've pared the list to the top three to five *key* points, the real fun begins as we challenge each other –

> "Who can tell a customer story that validates this claim about ease of use?"

> "Describe a scenario that dramatizes what we're calling the seamless integration of these new services."

> "OK – lets combine three features in a single story and make them come to life!"

As we begin to capture our stories, we give each one a title. We tell them to each other. We challenge various team members to either adapt or personalize a particular story or compose one from their direct experience that would serve the same purposes. Soon the team has developed a comprehensive storytelling strategy based on compelling and consistent content.

To give a concrete example, I worked with the Xbox team at Microsoft as they were preparing a new marketing campaign for the Xbox 360 videogame console. The campaign was slated to begin in the holiday selling season and continue through the following six to twelve months. The core marketing objective was to establish the Xbox 360 as an entertainment and media center for entire families, a vehicle for a wide variety of social experiences – not just a console for solitary hardcore videogame players.

In support of the objective, the company was introducing lots of new products and services, including a set of five family-oriented games bundled with the Xbox 360 console and called Xbox 360 Arcade, parental control software built into the console, new easier-to-use controllers, movie downloads from the online Xbox Live marketplace, and more.

It was a compelling line-up of products, features, and benefits. But in the form it had assumed – a typical message grid – was dull and lifeless. The challenge was to transform this laundry list of "messages" about a "product" into a set of stories that would enable the press, retailers, and consumers to see a new era of digital entertainment shared by families and friends, and all centered on the Xbox 360.

Once we went to the white board and opened the story room for business, that challenge quickly became a form of entertainment for the Microsoft team. By the end of the session, we had built two captivating, easy-to-tell stories that embodied all the key messages about the "new" Xbox 360.

The "holiday" story started with a grandmother buying the Xbox 360 Arcade bundle for her grandchildren and their parents as a holiday gift … went on to describe the family playing the five included games together … setting up the parental controls … listening to music from their Microsoft Zune player through the Xbox … connecting their Xbox Live Vision Camera and having a video web chat with their cousins thousands of miles away … watching a DVD on the Xbox, then downloading another movie from the Xbox Live service to watch the next day … and so on.

The "new year" story described the same family expanding their Xbox entertainment center with a hard drive … using it for DVD "movie nights" with family and friends … listening to podcasts … and building a library of games, videos, and other media to enjoy using their Xbox 360.

Communicating core values through storytelling. In business and the professions, your organization's core values are fundamental not only to the way you work but to the way you are seen, by your clients, customers, colleagues, and community. For example, my clients at Clif Bar Inc. proudly operate according to five distinct and distinctive business aspirations –

- Sustaining Our Brands
- Sustaining Our Community
- Sustaining Our People
- Sustaining Our Community
- Sustaining Our Planet

Talk to any employee of the company and the odds are very good he or she will have a story to tell about how their work is aligned with these aspirations.

That organization-wide understanding of and ability to articulate core values in stories is what makes them work for Clif Bar. Core values stories are like fertilizer – unless you spread them around they don't do much good. So let me tell a little story of my own …

Some years ago I led a workshop for a prestigious Silicon Valley law firm. This company of attorneys had grown rapidly during the technology boom of the 1990s, with numerous lateral hires and an expanding pool of young associates. But the members of the firm feared that, as an organization, they were beginning to lose their identity. They scheduled an offsite gathering to deal with the issue and asked me to facilitate one of the sessions.

My strategy, I told them, would be storytelling. A few eyebrows went up, but they signed on. So during the next week I conducted individual interviews with eight members of the firm: six senior partners, one lateral partner, and one associate. I focused on two tasks with each one. First, I asked each one to tell me stories about the firm, and together we mined the core values embedded in each story. Then, after settling on the story each one would tell at the offsite, I coached them as storytellers. We worked on structuring and telling the story for maximum effect, and on interpreting the story to highlight the core values it dramatized.

For the offsite, I gathered a collection of empty packing boxes and labeled each one, in large bold print, with one of the core values that was going to be brought to life through storytelling.

When the day came, the eight storytellers took the floor, one by one, and told their tales: about serving demanding clients, making difficult decisions, coming together in teams, going the extra mile, and more. While speaking, each one stacked the appropriate core values boxes at his or her side. At the end of each story, each one explained how the story represented those values – "And the moral of the story is…."

During the eight stories, I could tell that the "audience" was really engaged by what they were hearing and seeing, and at the end I was satisfied that the session had delivered good value to my client. But then something remarkable happened. In a flurry of pure improvisation, another five members of the firm stood up and told specific, detailed, even colorful stories that highlighted some of the same core values they'd just heard about and even unearthed some more.

The evaluations of the session confirmed that it had made a major impact on all participants – that storytelling had helped restore their sense of identity as an organization and would help them communicate that to others:

- "Now I know who we are."
- "This gives me such a sense of pride."
- "Thank you for reminding me why the work we do is so important."
- "This will help me so much in pitching the firm."
- "Now I own these stories and I plan to tell them."

And the moral of the story is this: Every organization can use storytelling both to *discover* its core values and to bring them to life and put them to use.

The storytelling organization knows what makes *itself*, as well as its products and services, special, and its members have a powerful set of tools for communicating that to others both inside and outside. The trick is to establish organized ways of unearthing and sharing your stories. To kick-start the effort, it's often helpful to bring in someone to facilitate a storytelling session like the ones I've described.

But there are other ways to promote the telling of stories across your organization. You might make time at regular meetings for departments or working teams to share stories of a recent challenge or milestone. You might create a storytelling space, a section in the employee newsletter, a wiki or a blog, where people are encouraged to share and comment on stories about the life and history of the organization and its offerings.

When it's showtime, tell it with a story!

Chapter 8
Putting It Together:
A Foolproof Blueprint for Structuring Any Presentation

The previous three chapters are about creating and using the tools and materials that go into an effective presentation: messages that have the fine, rich intensity of a master chef's sauce … powerbites that drive your messages home like the sure, true blows of a hammer … and the ways you can use stories to bring your message and your mission to life and connect with the hearts and minds of your audience.

Now, what's the most effective way to put them together?

The Importance of Structure

Consider the presentations you've attended. Think how often the speaker's idea of structure seemed to be *start talking and go on and on until time runs out.* Think of the PowerPoint presentations that ended in halting embarrassment as the speaker ran out of slides before running out of time or, for that matter, before making a point. Or – even worse – the presentations when the speaker ran out of time before running out of slides, and left the audience wondering, "What did we miss?"

Even when a speaker manages to deliver all the slides, at a consistent pace and within the allotted time, PowerPoint often lures a presentation into a linear procession to nowhere. The audience is treated to a succession of slides, adding up to a list of things that must be important – otherwise, they wouldn't have been featured on slides, right? The problem is, no one thing seems any more important than any other. There's no sense of progression, little emphasis, few logical signposts. The audience is left wondering, "What was the point?"

(Of course, any presentation, PowerPoint or not, can drift. My point here is not to dump on PowerPoint. It can be a very useful tool, and, in any case, it's here to stay.)

Every audience wants structure. You might even say that, like children, every audience *needs* structure. In any case, as a presenter you owe it to your audience to *provide* structure. Structure helps them listen and keeps them listening. Structure does more than enable you to organize your presentation; by enabling your audience to organize your presentation in their minds, structure helps them understand and remember it.

"Say What You're Going to Say …"

This chapter is about structure, not content. Your particular purpose – exactly what you want to persuade your audience to believe or to do – will always drive the content of your presentation. A trial summation is different from a sales pitch is different from a press briefing is different from a conference keynote. For that matter, every trial summation, sales pitch, press briefing, and conference keynote is different from every other presentation of the same genre.

So I can't lay out some one-size-fits-all way to organize your thoughts. What I can offer is a foolproof blueprint for two of the three basic structural elements of a presentation: the beginning and the end. The middle, being the substance of what you have to say, is up to you. But the beauty of this approach is, even if you haven't already got a thorough grasp on the substance of your presentation, this blueprint will both force you and help you to do so.

When we were learning to write, most of us were taught this fundamental way to organize an essay: Say what you're going to say … say it … then say what you've said. Tried and true, this is in fact the basis for my blueprint for effective presentations.

The Opening

As proverbial wisdom and our parents would have us remember, first impressions are powerful and persistent. So you will not be surprised to read that the opening of any presentation is crucial for several reasons.

First and foremost, this is the moment when your audience is most attentive. Research shows that people's attention is keenest during the first few minutes of a presentation. In as little as five minutes, that attention begins to sag – and then it usually goes downhill from there. You simply cannot afford to squander those first precious minutes. And there is much to do during them.

Your opening is your chance to capture the audience's attention and establish rapport with them. There is no more effective way to do that than to answer what I've identified, in an earlier chapter, as the foremost question in the minds of every audience: *What's in it for me?* You can define the answer in your opening or, more tantalizingly, suggest it. Either way, self-interest is the most powerful motivator in the world; by appealing to theirs, you will compel your audience to listen attentively to what you have to say.

I believe it's just as important to outline or at least preview your presentation in your opening. By telling an audience where you're going and what to expect, you make them partners in the journey. In effect, you coach them in how to listen to your presentation.

Finally, the opening is a good time to establish your message mantra. Don't be afraid of "giving away the end" of your speech. Instead, remind yourself of the lamentable fact that many people are likely to leave the room before you reach your big conclusion; you don't want them to get away without hearing the single most important thing you want them to remember. Remember, too, that a key function of your message mantra is to unify your presentation in the minds of the audience. Like telling them what to expect, your message mantra serves the audience as an aid to listening and a foundation for understanding your entire presentation.

To achieve these objectives, your opening needs to contain three essential elements that I call *the hook, the promise, and the roadmap.*

The hook is all about one objective: seizing your audience's attention. The hook can come in any number of shapes and sizes. For example, you can cite and comment on a current news headline ... ask a rhetorical question ... unveil something new ... present a unique visual ... or share some unexpected or surprising data.

As you might expect after reading the last chapter, I tend to favor the storytelling hook, because of its power to capture not only the audience's attention but their imagination, too. I've seen storytelling work its magic in the opening of many presentations, including these ...

In an unforgettable debut before a national audience, a healthcare executive opened with the story of a pediatrician in his organization who was presented with a child in imminent danger from a difficult-to-diagnose heart condition. Masterfully composed and delivered, this compelling narrative captivated the audience while dramatizing all of the key characteristics of the healthcare model the speaker advocated.

The story followed the doctor as he rushed down the hall to consult with a specialist (integrated care) ... used advanced computer search technology to diagnose the child's condition as a life-threatening emergency (technology innovation) ... and called for a Medevac to transport the patient to a special facility (centers of excellence). The story ended on a heart-warming note as the doctor made his annual visit to his former patient's birthday party. In less than five minutes, the executive had the audience firmly in his grasp, as he went on to observe that there are thousands of such doctors and such stories in his organization, empowered by a healthcare model that delivers superior care while inspiring pride among the providers.

I once worked with a client who was preparing a presentation for executives on professional ethics. For his hook, he decided to read, word for word, from a newspaper story. The risk of starting off by reading from a text – what could be duller? – was counterbalanced by the drama and authenticity of the story, which described in graphic, harrowing detail a prominent executive's fall from grace. Having captured the audience's attention, he then posed the question: "Could this happen to you?" Talk about a "what's-in-it-for-me" bombshell! From that moment, the speaker had the undivided attention of everyone in the room.

Another client used an aspirational story – what I call "the nirvana hook" – to open a presentation on project management. He painted a vivid picture of a company succeeding, thriving, and growing by harnessing its business processes to a unique new model of project management. Having hooked his audience with this tantalizing slice of the organizational life of the future, the speaker had their full attention – and in the end, their buy-in – as he went on to describe how such "nirvana" could be achieved.

My final example of a compelling hook comes from a case of what I call *presenting up* – that is, making an internal presentation to your management. A pair of business professionals was scheduled to appear before the executive committee of a large organization in order to secure final buy-in for a major technology project. A lot of groundwork had been done in the preceding months, and the pair was concerned they might open a Pandora's Box of issues if they reviewed the whole history and the many decisions that had led to this important moment.

With the blessing of their sponsor (always important when presenting up), they chose instead to open with a unique hook: they read a letter, supposedly from the executive committee itself to the entire company, announcing the committee's support for the initiative, outlining the reasons for it, and describing what would be expected of everyone in the organization in support of the project. This unique hook, which actually constituted pretty much the entire presentation, worked like a charm. After a few questions, the executive committee members gave their blessing and thanked the pair of presenters for both the project and the brevity of their presentation.

What about using a joke as your hook? I strongly advise against it. When Sir Donald Wolfit, a renowned British stage actor, was on his deathbed, a young colleague said to him, "Sir Donald, after a life so filled with success and fame, dying must hard." "Dying is easy," replied the aged thespian, "*comedy* is hard." If comedy is difficult for actors (and I can testify that it is), it's even harder for the average speaker. It's especially risky to try to be funny at the beginning of a presentation, before the audience has gotten a sense of your personality, timing, and vocal style.

The rewards of opening with a joke, long shot that they are, hardly seem worth the risk. If your joke bombs, you can easily lose your audience for good, right out of the gate. And really, what's to be gained? "I'm a funny person" is an essential hook in a stand-up comedy routine. But rarely, if ever, will it be the first thing you need to establish in a business or professional presentation. Humor can be great for livening up a presentation or reviving an audience that's losing focus. But hold off on the jokes until you're relaxed and comfortable with your audience and they with you.

The promise is your explicit answer to the question *What's in it for me?* By describing the insights, capabilities, and other benefits that the audience will gain from your presentation, you offer your commitment to the audience to repay them for listening — and you deepen their commitment to doing just that.

Here are a few opening promises used by clients I've worked with:

> "When we're finished, you'll have all the tools you need to make sound ethical judgments you can count on to protect you from litigation."

> "At the end of this presentation, you'll understand how a transformation of our organizational culture from technology-focused to entertainment-focused will guarantee our future."

> "My goal is to inspire you to share my enthusiasm for our doctor empanelment initiative. When you leave this room, you'll understand the quality-of-care benefits, you'll see how easy we make it for you to participate, and you'll appreciate how this initiative will enhance not only patient satisfaction, but your own as well"

> "Through this presentation I hope to persuade you of the incredible value of teaming with project management experts when pitching new commercial building clients."

The roadmap serves as an agenda for the audience. The roadmap backs up the promise by outlining how you're going to fulfill it. By giving your audience a sense of the scope of the journey ahead and the route you plan to take, the roadmap allows them to buckle in more securely. By giving them an outline or preview of topics and ideas to listen for, the roadmap enables them to be better listeners.

The typical roadmap is pretty straightforward, short and simple, as it should be. Here are three examples I've heard in my practice:

"First, we'll survey the legal landscape, and I'll offer you some tools to calibrate your ethical compass. Next, we'll look at a few compelling case studies. And finally, I will address one issue that I *know* is of special interest to you."

"I first want to frame this issue in the context of our other quality and service initiatives. Then I'll show you some compelling data on the impact of improved access. Next, I'll describe our initiative in detail, with special attention to your role. And finally, I'll show you how far this initiative can go in improving *your* long-term satisfaction."

"My roadmap is simple. First, I'll show how we can sweeten the pitch. Next, we'll describe some examples of how we can accelerate every project, which means getting you to your commission faster. Finally, we'll explore various ways of deepening and extending your relationship with the client."

"Say It . . .": The Roadmap and the Core

As the examples illustrate, the roadmap is a summary. With the roadmap, you *say what you're going to say*. Then, of course, you *say it,* which is the core of your presentation. That's what makes the roadmap such a valuable tool for you as well as the audience. And you can use this tool in more than one way, depending on how you go about preparing your presentation.

If you haven't already planned and organized what you're going to say, composing your roadmap will force you to do so. In effect, you'll use the roadmap as an outline.

Or you may flesh out the core of your presentation first. Then preparing your roadmap can serve as checkpoint. Summarizing your presentation in the simple, straightforward, and brief form of a roadmap is a great way of asking yourself if it's clear, coherent, and complete.

The Close: "Say What You've Said"

The close is not the close only in the sense of *the end* – it's when you *close the deal* with your audience.

In the close you connect all the dots. You drive home your message mantra. And you issue a call to action – at least a call to believe – to your audience.

In the close, according to the old essay-writing blueprint, you *say what you've said.* To do that – and to accommodate the inevitable latecomers who may have missed your brilliant opening and even part of the core of your presentation – I recommend a simple strategy: recapitulate the key elements of your opening.

By returning to the hook you used in the opening, you can unify your presentation and give the audience a sense of closure. A few examples:

> "And so we return to Maria, the patient whose story opened this presentation. Hers is just one story of the huge difference our new model of patient care can make. And I trust you believe, just as I do, that this is just the beginning …"

> "I opened today by reading you a newspaper headline that chronicled the devastation of a career just like yours. With the knowledge and tools I've shared with you here, I believe you can make sure that you are never the subject of such a news story."

> "One memorable day on a mountain, it took a team to rescue my father-in-law from the crevasse that threatened to be his grave. Not a single hero, but all the climbers on that mountain, working together — just as, *together,* we can take this enterprise to the next level."

By reminding your audience of the promise, you lay it on the line. You say, in effect, "I made a promise and I'm not afraid to repeat it because I'm confident that I've delivered." Some examples:

> "I promised when I began today that by the end of the session, you would share my enthusiasm for this initiative … that you would see the huge impact it will have on the quality of our care and service … and that you would understand how easy it will be for you to participate."

> "I promised you earlier that I was going to show you how changing our focus from a technology-driven platform to an entertainment-driven platform will ensure our future and guarantee our success."

> "I promised you that you would see the immense benefit of teaming with project management as you engage clients seeking new commercial facilities."

Reviewing the roadmap is a succinct way to *say what you've said* in the core of your presentation. For example:

> "You've come to understand and appreciate the hazards of the climate you work in. You've heard about the latest in both case law and policies and procedures. You've done a helpful self-assessment of vulnerabilities. I've shared with you some strategies, tactics, and tips that you can apply today. And along the way we've been able

to look in some detail at some compelling case studies as a means of sharpening both your awareness and your skills."

"I've laid out the reasons our competitiveness and success depend on our quality and service initiatives. You've seen some compelling data on the impact of improved access. You understand the details of our newest initiative and of your role. Finally, I trust you now see how empanelment will secure our long-term future as physicians."

There's one more reason to invoke any or all of the elements that made up your opening when you're drawing things to a close. Doing so is a great way to signal the audience that you — and they — are approaching the end. Signaling them that you're "finishing up" will almost always revive the flagging spirits and sharpen the attention of an audience. But always take special care as you approach the end of your presentation. If you tip off the audience too soon that you're coming to a close, they may start to pack up and psychically or physically leave the room. On the other and, if you put in several "false endings" — that is, indicate that you're concluding a number of times without actually doing so — you're likely to annoy your audience and leave them with the impression that you're a windbag.

Make It Yours

Every speech or presentation is unique, as it should be. In the end, how you organize it has to work for you, for the occasion and purpose of the presentation, and, of course, for your audience. I've called the ideas in this chapter a blueprint, but you should consider them a rough drawing.

As I've noted, for example, there are all kinds of ways to hook an audience. Oftentimes, the promise and the roadmap can easily be combined — indeed, sometimes it only makes sense to combine them. On some occasions, the whole point may be to build to a big announcement, a dramatic conclusion, or a surprise; in these cases you won't want to give anything away, so you'll omit the promise or the roadmap altogether.

Similarly, it's up to you to use, arrange, and emphasize the elements of your close in the way that works best. Weaving together the return to the hook, the promise, and the roadmap is an art. And as with any art, you want your audience to experience the art and not the technique. Sometimes it may make sense to bring in something altogether new at the close — new information or a fresh story or anecdote — in order to make your close that much more compelling.

And so in structuring this chapter, I return to the beginning. Structure does more than enable you to organize your presentation; by enabling your audience to organize your presentation in their minds, structure helps them understand and remember it.

Part III:
Mastering Your Craft as a Communicator

Chapter 9
The Power of the Voice

The most compelling public speakers, the best actors, the greatest "pitch" masters, all have one thing in common: great use of the voice.

Note that I don't say "a great voice." Voices vary infinitely, and the one nature gave you is the one you have to work with. You may not be blessed with the great "pipes" of a Richard Burton or a Lauren Bacall, but no matter; you can use the voice you have to great effect. In talking, as in most everything else, there are certain techniques for getting the most out of your natural ability.

My aim in this chapter is simply to make you aware of the basic techniques for controlling and varying your use of your voice. Vocalization is a physical, even athletic activity, and like any sport, it can take many hours of practice and years of experience to master. This is one part of my coaching curriculum that usually involves a practicum; just as you can't learn to sing by reading music, you can't develop your vocal style and power by simply reading about vocal techniques. Nevertheless, I've seen many clients improve their public speaking by leaps and bounds simply by being aware of the quality of their own voices, how they're using them, and the basic options they have for using them better.

Projection: Supporting Your Voice

Just as we often speak of the quality of a voice as its "color" or "character," we employ even more elaborate metaphorical language to describe voices. How would you describe your best friend's voice, or your spouse's, or your own? Is it bright or breathy, silky or smoky, smooth or raw, resonant or reedy, bell-like or booming?

The fundamental distinction is weak or strong. Strong is better; no matter what the inherent character of your voice, you always bring out its best qualities, and sound more confident and more persuasive, by using it vigorously. In the theater, this is called *projection*.

Projection is more than just a matter of how loud you are. A good actor or speaker can actually lower his or her voice (or at least seem to) and be heard in the farthest row of the balcony. Projection is a matter of supporting your voice with your breath. It comes from your diaphragm, the musculature that operates your lungs. That's why it's important to be aware of your breathing when you're speaking in public. Being mindful of your breathing will help you take deep, full breaths, which will in turn keep you from hurrying your speech and running out of breath. Before long, you'll get in the habit of supporting your voice with good breathing, and it will become natural to you.

Projection is also a matter of where your voice comes from inside your head, throat, and chest. Learning to "place" your voice requires the guidance of a vocal coach or at least a self-teaching audio program. But in general, the further "back" a voice comes from, the more it fills the oral cavity and throat, the stronger it will project.

One simple tip that most amateur actors and singers learn: When you're giving a presentation, always talk to the *last row* of the audience. Making a conscious effort to do so will automatically improve your projection.

Articulation: The Art of Being Understood

Americans are notoriously lazy speakers. This is not just a matter of how idiomatic and slangy our modern American version of English has become. Much of the crispness of traditional English pronunciation has gone by the wayside in our everyday communications. (Of course, if you learn a foreign language from a textbook or a bunch of audio tapes, then go to the country where it's spoken, you'll probably think the natives there are a tribe of mushmouths, too.)

You can't deliver an effective presentation – people will simply stop paying attention to you – if you can't be understood. Pronouncing words clearly, known as articulation or diction, is essential to your power of persuasion. The kind of lazy talking we can get away with in our personal and everyday communications – the consonants soft and blurry, the vowels clipped or jumped over – can quickly undermine your effectiveness as a public speaker. Especially if you tend to talk fast, or if you find that people often ask you to repeat yourself, consider your diction at risk.

Good diction depends on the full, supple use of the whole speaking apparatus: lips, teeth, tongue, and jaw. Improving your articulation requires training and practice, usually with the help of a vocal coach or audio program. But you can make a start on improving your diction by being mindful of how fast you're talking, slowing down if necessary, and taking care to "finish off" each of the sounds that make up every word – especially the words at the beginning and end of each sentence.

Volume, Pitch, Pace, Cadence: The Music of Speech

The human voice really is like a musical instrument or even a complete ensemble. It can run nimbly through an enormous range of notes … blare like a trumpet and purr like a cello … march briskly through a string of syllables or caress a lonely word … pound out a dirge and boogie like a ragtime tune … bring us to our feet like an anthem or put us to sleep like a lullaby. And our language gives us an infinite range of music to play.

With the mastery they have of their vocal instruments, great actors let us hear all that music, especially when they're performing the works of Shakespeare and other masters of poetic, theatrical language. But the same tricks and techniques great actors use are available to all of us; in fact, we use them every day.

Volume is the favorite vocal tool for many if not most speakers. After all, raising the voice or "punching up" a word or phrase with a burst of greater volume is the most natural way of getting attention or emphasizing a point. Unfortunately, many American speakers seem to regard *louder* as their only vocal technique. The other end of volume control – lowering your voice, speaking softly or even in a whisper – is an enormously effective way to draw an audience toward you. The next time you're listening to a practiced public speaker, watch your fellow audience members when the speaker lowers the volume. You'll see people literally leaning forward in their seats, and you'll probably also notice them becoming quieter as well.

Pitch, a term borrowed directly from music, describes a vocal dimension that we learn to use before we learn to make sentences. A toddler may not know all the words he needs or how to string them together into a request, but by raising the pitch of his voice at the end of the sound he makes, he lets us know that he's asking a question (or, more likely, asking for something he wants).

Inflection is a change in pitch applied to a single word. Inflections are very effective vocal techniques for adding meaning or force to particular words. A *downward inflection* – a word that starts at one pitch and then goes down – has power and authority and also implies finality. An *upward inflection* – a word that starts at one pitch and then goes up at the end – can not only ask a question, like the toddler; it can also create a sense of drama, tension, and anticipation.

A series of upward inflections, a technique I call the *stairway to heaven*, works great when you're listing things. A *circumflexed* word is one that is pitched first up, then down, or down-up, or even up-down-up. Words that have special contextual meaning or are being used to paint a picture are often circumflexed.

Whatever kind of music you like, part of what pleases you about it is the range of tempos and rhythms you hear, whether you're listening to a symphony, a suite, or a single song. Spoken language offers the same pleasures and the same opportunities to use *pace*, the speed of your talking, and *cadence*, the rhythmic flow of your words, to add to the interest, the meaning, and the force of what you say.

Consider, for example, a good storyteller or even just someone who tells a joke well. A good deal of his mastery lies in the way he controls and varies pace and cadence to match the various moments and movements of the story, from exposition to dramatic conflict, climax, and resolution.

In everyday life, how fast someone talks gives us a plethora of signals about what he or she is saying – its meaning, its urgency or importance, how the speaker feels about it, and more. Likewise, the cadence of speech can captivate us or bore us. Much English poetry, including the plays of Shakespeare, follows the cadence of iambic pentameter: a line of five iambs, each one made up of an unstressed syllable followed by a stressed syllable (da-DUM). For example:

> When *I* do *count* the *clock* that *tells* the *time* ...
>   (the opening line of Shakespeare's Sonnet 12)
> Is *this* the *face* that *launched* a *thou*sand *ships*?
>   (the famous line about Helen of Troy in Marlowe's
>   play, *Dr. Faustus)*
> Made *weak* by *time* and *fate*, but *strong* in *will*
> To *strive*, to *seek*, to *find*, and *not* to *yield*.
>   (the last two lines of Tennyson's poem, "Ulysses")

The modern American playwright David Mamet has observed that iambic pentameter is actually the natural cadence of spoken English, including the highly idiomatic and often profane dialogue he writes for his own plays. In any case, it is the skillful *variations* in cadence that distinguishes the art of Shakespeare and other great poets and playwrights. Listening to an endless march of pure iambic pentameter, or any other regularly cadenced language, would put us to sleep if it didn't drive us crazy first.

"Variety is the spice of the spoken word" is a lesson every speaker must learn – and it applies to all the dimensions of vocalization. In volume, pitch, pace, and cadence, *variety* is your greatest ally. Keep in mind how we describe a speaker who has bored us. We say that "she *droned*" – meaning that her voice seemed never to vary in volume or pitch. Or, saying that "he went *on* and *on*" or spoke in a *singsong* way, we mimic (and ridicule) the unvaried cadence that made it seem like the speaker had no feeling for what he or she was saying – and would never finish.

As a final note on the music of speech, I'd like to put in a word about *no words*. In my experience, *the pause* is the most overlooked and neglected oratorical tool among all but the most expert business and professional presenters. Silence is enormously powerful. It can bring the wandering attention of an audience back to you. It can underline the last thing you said, or build anticipation for the next thing you say. It can even get a laugh.

Mastering the music of speech is a matter of long practice. As with real music, it takes a well-trained ear in addition to a well-tuned instrument. But, just as with real music, you don't have to play everything from memory. In the theater, actors commonly mark up their scripts with various performance notes while they're rehearsing and memorizing their lines. They might underline certain words they want to emphasize or treat in some other special way ... make a note about their intentions with a certain line ... and use notations for passages where they want to pause, accelerate, or slow down, turn up the volume or lower it. Especially when you're going to be presenting from a verbatim script (on paper or a teleprompter), you can "score" your script in the same way.

Speaking Into the Microphone

Most of us have had the excruciating experience of watching and listening as a speaker fought with a microphone and lost. The tall one who hunched over and twisted his head unnaturally in an effort to make contact with the audience, because the mike was too low and he didn't take the time, or know how, to raise it. The one who manhandled the mike or chewed on it, making explosive sounds that jarred both the audience and himself. The one who stood back, intimidated by the device yet trusting it to carry her message, when all the while the mike, let alone the audience, had no chance of picking up her too-soft voice.

In short, a microphone can present you with a classic victor-versus-victim choice. Will you use it to your advantage or be defeated by it?

Microphones come in many varieties — on a stand, attached to a lectern (usually by a flexible neck), hand-held, hung around your neck or clipped to your lapel – and if public speaking is part of your professional life, you'll probably have to deal with each kind someday. A couple of tips: When using a mike on a stand or lectern, adjust it so that it's about six to ten inches from your face and below your chin. A lavaliere or clip-on mike should be placed about six inches below your chin and at or close to the center at your sternum (if it's pinned aside on one lapel, every time you turn your head the other way your voice will fade out).

In any case, remember that a microphone is designed to pick up your voice as it travels *toward the audience*. Speak to them, not to the mike. Talk just as you would if you didn't have a microphone, and let the technician monitoring the sound system adjust the volume to you. Just avoid hitting your consonants too hard, especially those popping *p*'s.

Taking Care of Your Voice

When practicing your vocal technique, rehearsing a presentation, or just in the everyday use of your voice, it's important to take care of it. Talking is hard work, and voices get tired just like any other organ that's used so much. When you feel your voice getting raw or raspy, when your jaws start to ache or your lungs start to feel tired, stop and be quiet, and give your vocal instrument a rest.

Actors are notorious for the variety of their voice remedies. They range from the simple, mild tea and a bit of honey and lemon, to the extreme, bags full of lozenges and supplements. If and when you're having trouble with your voice, I suggest the following steps:

- Make sure you're supporting your voice with your lungs. Think of your voice box as the light bulb and your diaphragm as the power plant.

- Get some vocal rest. Silence is a great healer. But don't think you're sparing your voice by whispering! Whispering is actually very hard on the vocal chords.

- Breathe steam. Take the long hot shower or place a towel over your head and breathe from a bowl of steaming hot water. Or simply breathe the steam from a cup of tea, preferably Throat Coat. Among lozenges, I've found those containing zinc are most effective.

The day before a big presentation, see if you can take more "quiet time" than usual to give your voice some rest; in any case, don't go to a concert or sporting event and scream your lungs out. And before going on in front of your audience, always give your voice a chance to warm up, either with a set of vocal exercises or by rehearsing a portion of your speech.

Exercise

"Umm ... uh ... like ... you know": Verbal Tics and How to Cure Them

We've, umm, all sat through the, you know, kind of presentation that gets, like, unbearable because the speaker just can't, you know, stop sticking *umms* and *uhs* and *likes* and other junk into every sentence or idea. These habitual verbal tics are sometimes rooted in problems with content, preparation, or confidence. But if you're afflicted, you need not despair – there is a cure.

Sit down with a trusted friend, colleague, or family member and start talking. You can run through a presentation you've done before, describe your plans for one that you have coming up, or just talk about a recent event. But before you begin, make a contract with your audience of one that he or she will interrupt with a loud buzzing sound or snap of the fingers *every time* you say "umm" or "you know" or the like.

Warning: As you're interrupted again and again, you will be aghast at how often you fall back on your tics. You may get upset, even angry, and lose your train of thought more than once. But keep at it. As your awareness of them grows, so will your concentration on suppressing your tics. You'll find that you need to slow down and think ahead. At first, you will probably have to "stop yourself" and replace each "umm" and "uh" with a brief pause.

Break down what you're saying into units, or sets of ideas, and try to get through one at a time without a single tic. You'll soon be on your way to success. But don't rely on a single such session to cure you. You must remain vigilant about your tic. Ask those you trust to remind you when you slip. You should be able to completely purge your communications of all verbal tics in three to six weeks.

Chapter 10
Producing, Designing, and Directing Your Presentation

In the theater, all kinds of things go on before the show and behind the scenes to create what the audience sees and hears on the stage during the show. The producer and her staff raise the money, buy the rights to the play, rent the theater, and hire the cast and crew … the director shapes the work of the actors, through a series of rehearsals, into a coherent and compelling enactment of the script … set, lighting, and sound designers create the onstage world where the play will take place … costume designers, makeup artists, dialogue coaches, and others ensure that each actor looks and sounds the part he or she is playing … and an army of carpenters, electricians, riggers, seamstresses, stage managers, and other technicians build the complex apparatus of the production and run it all from behind the scenes each night.

Well, guess what? When it's "Your Show, Created by You, Presented by You, Starring You," most if not all of these tasks fall on you. You are the producer, designer, and director as well as the star performer. To set yourself up for success in every presentation, you have to take responsibility for all these roles.

You the Producer

As a producer, you have to think about all the elements of the space where your show will take place, including—

- the seating and sight lines
- the acoustics and sound system
- the lighting and visuals, from programs (usually called handouts in business presentations) to PowerPoint or video
- all the elements that will affect the comfort of the audience, from the ambient temperature to refreshments and restrooms

In some venues, such as conference facilities or dedicated meeting rooms, many of these elements may be in place. You may even be familiar with them from previous events. But I caution against taking *anything* for granted.

Always preview the space where you'll be presenting. Look at the setup and seating configuration. Will it serve your presentation well? Will everyone be able to see you and everything else that you want them to see (PowerPoint, product demo, video)? Can you change the setup more to your liking?

For example, just because the chairs are in rows doesn't mean they have to be; maybe you'd prefer to have your audience seated in a semicircle so that they're aware of each other as well as of you. Just because the room has a stage at one end with a lectern and a fixed microphone doesn't mean you have to speak from there; maybe you can arrange to use a remote microphone that will allow you to roam the stage, or the entire room, for a more dynamic physical presence during your presentation.

When showing PowerPoint slides as part of your presentation, do not place the projection screen in the center of the stage or end of the room where you'll be presenting if you can avoid it. Instead, place the screen on your left (the audience's right) and keep center stage for yourself. That way, you will be the star while your slides play a supporting role.

When giving a presentation at an unfamiliar venue, get there ahead of time. Become familiar with the equipment you'll be relying on – microphones, teleprompter, overhead projector, laptop computer, and so forth – and the people you'll be relying on to operate that equipment.

Think through all the technical aspects of your presentation, then make plans for having things go wrong. Are your PowerPoint visuals absolutely essential to communicating what you have to say? Then you might want to bring printed copies just in case the projector goes down. Will you be delivering a verbatim speech from a teleprompter? Teleprompters have been known to fail, so carry a printed copy in your pocket.

As the producer of your presentation, be firm about the things you can control, flexible about those you can't, and wise enough to recognize the difference. You may have to make changes, even at the last minute, to what you plan to present and how it's presented. But it's better to do some last-minute scrambling than to become the victim of an awkward presentation space, unreliable equipment, or untoward events.

Designing Yourself for Success

Appearance counts – and communicates. That's why, on the stage, the villain is clad in black, brides wear white, and the innocent young ingénue *doesn't* come onstage in a scarlet cocktail dress. As the designer of your show, you're responsible for the "look" of everything the audience sees, starting with yourself.

It's not just a matter of being well groomed, but *how* you are groomed. Remember, you are a character in a show; what you wear is your costume, and it tells the audience something about you the moment they set eyes on you. Some leadership coaches now advise their business and professional clients to use the way they dress – say, a signature color or distinctive accessory – to establish a "personal brand." What will your costume say about your personal brand when it's showtime?

Steve Jobs can get away with the jeans-and-black-turtleneck look, even at a shareholders' meeting, but you probably cannot. Will you benefit from the strength and solidity of a pinstripe suit, or will an open-collar shirt and a sport coat be more appealing to your audience? If you're petite, will a "power color" like red add to your stature and authority onstage? What will you be *expected* to wear, and is it best to meet expectations or do you want to make a statement by pushing the envelope a bit?

In general, women have more choices to make about their appearance than men. I advise all my clients to avoid clothing with a complicated or "loud" design, dangling jewelry, or other distracting accessories. By distracting the eyes of your listeners, you can also distract their ears and torpedo your presentation.

The baseline is, your costume should be appropriate to the occasion and the venue and, ideally, flattering to your physique and your natural coloring. Above all, it should be something you feel comfortable in, because the more comfortable you are the more relaxed and confident you will be as well.

Directing Yourself

In the first of the presidential debates of 2004, incumbent president George W. Bush's performance earned mediocre reviews at best, even from his partisans. This was clearly on his mind when he was asked later what he had learned from the "strong women" in his life, notably his wife. "Stand up straight and don't scowl," he said. Evidently, Mrs. Bush had not minced words with him.

Hers was good advice for any speaker. With our reliance on language, we humans tend to forget the importance of nonverbal cues and just how much they influence what we think and feel. When you appear in front of an audience to make a presentation, you speak with far more than your voice. Your posture, movements, gestures, and facial expressions communicate plenty. We call it "body language" for good reason, and it can either enhance or undermine the power and even the meaning of your spoken words.

Actors are trained in the use of their bodies as well as their voices. You may be more or less aware of how you carry yourself, your posture and movements and gestures; in general, people who have trained in a sport or in any kind of dance are more "body aware." In addition, actors always have a director to tell them where to enter and exit, where to walk and stand, when to sit – even, sometimes, *how* to stand, *how* to sit, *how* to use their hands, and so forth. As a presenter, you can't count on having the benefit of such a resource.

So you have to direct yourself as a performer – and train yourself. To that end, here are a few basic directorial tricks and techniques I teach my clients, which you can put into practice on your own.

Your "Money" Positions

This is yet one more reason you should reconnoiter the venue before delivering a presentation. And take a friend or colleague with you, because you'll need someone to look at you from the audience's point of view.

Your mission: to find three "money" positions within the performance space, places to stand or sit and ways of holding yourself in each place that make you feel comfortable and help you look relaxed but authoritative. These money positions will draw your audience toward you and command their attention.

As your colleague looks on, try a number of positions within the space. You may find that anchoring yourself to a physical object is comforting and helpful. Try leaning on the lectern, standing with your hand on a chair, writing at the white board, leaning or half-sitting on a the edge of a table. Don't be surprised if the toughest position of all is simply standing in the middle of the stage or the room with *nothing* to hold on to – that's the scariest position for most people.

At each position, take time to adjust your posture until you feel that you "own" the space. Get feedback from your colleague. Which of your profiles, left or right, looks better? What if you shift your weight, or cross one leg in front of the other? Do you lose "presence" when you sit, or gain power? Ask your colleague, when you find a position and posture that makes you look like a million bucks, to call out, "Money!" Then keep exploring and find at least two more.

These three positions, where you know you're comfortable and look great, will serve as your home base or security zone during your presentation. You'll be able to use any or all of them as a source of confidence and comfort. Your money positions can also serve as your "itinerary": if you do nothing more than move from one to another during the course of your presentation, your performance will gain in dynamism, energy, and confident command of your audience.

The Power of Gesture

Of the many people I've watched making public presentations, most come off as lacking in energy (not to say, lifeless) because they neglect to project themselves as vital, animated human beings. They fail to exploit the power of gesture, and as a result they tend to shrink within the space around them rather than dominate it.

We know and use the power of gesture constantly and instinctively in our everyday lives. We use gestures to draw pictures in the air, to emphasize or editorialize on things we say, and to communicate how we feel about what we say. We are naturally fluent in the rich language of gesture, on both the sending and the receiving end.

As the director of yourself and your presentation, you have to deal with two issues regarding your use of gesture. First, if you're the kind of person who tends to freeze up and become afraid to gesture when speaking in public, you have to learn to loosen up and reclaim the persuasive power of gesture. In the next chapter on rehearsing, I describe a technique that can help you do so.

You also have to pay attention to the *scale* of your gesturing, and make sure it suits the space where you're presenting. It's like the difference, for actors, between acting in front of a camera or on the stage, or between acting in a theater that seats 100 and one that seats 3,000.

When you're making a presentation in a small meeting room or on video, gestures on an everyday scale will be perfectly expressive and natural. But in a medium-sized conference room or small auditorium, you have to turn up the scale and energy of your gestures. In a large auditorium or similar space, you have to make your gestures grand indeed – literally "bigger than life." This may feel unnatural at first and take some getting used to. But rest assured that, in a large space, gestures that may seem over the top to you as a presenter will read as both clear and natural to your audience.

Where Are You Going – and Why?

In the theater it's called blocking – the movement of each actor on the stage, moment by moment – and it is meticulously devised and executed by the director and actors to clarify and enrich the meaning of the play. In a presentation, too, movement can clarify and enrich the meaning of what's being said while adding overall energy and variety. But just as in the theater, your movements must be planned and practiced.

To start with, your movements as a presenter must be *purposeful*. As a coach, I've dealt with my share of frenetic presenters. Somewhere along the line these lost souls got the idea that dynamic presenting means constant movement. So they wander continuously as they talk, as if a moving target is the most compelling thing an audience has ever seen. On the contrary, the wandering talker is both distracting and frustrating to an audience. They're so busy watching that they forget to listen, until they realize that the speaker's perpetual motion doesn't mean anything, and by then they've lost the thread.

So when you're devising your own blocking for a presentation, it's important to think about not only where you're going but why. Here are a few pointers:

Move on transitions. Virtually every speech or presentation has at least a few key transitions and pivot points. These are ideal moments to move. By changing your position, you can both signal and complement a change of subject or tone, a shift from past to present or present to future, a broadening of perspective or a raising of the stakes.

The strolling (not wandering) storyteller. Maybe because stories themselves have a kind of kinetic energy, movement and storytelling go well together. If your presentation includes a story or two (and I hope it does), use them to go for a stroll, but don't simply walk about aimlessly. Decide when to start moving, where you want to finish the story, and when and where – in the story and the performance space – you want to stop and anchor yourself and the audience, if only for a moment.

The power of stillness. Every good actor and stage director knows that a pause in the midst of movement, a sudden moment of stillness, can be as powerful as a pause in speaking. Especially when you're building to a conclusion or a call to action, you can use movement to raise the energy level; but for the moment or statement of vital importance, try standing perfectly still. Think of stillness as shining a spotlight, on you and your message.

Don't Plan on "Winging It"

As both director and actor, you have complete control over and responsibility for all the details of your performance: your money positions, gestures, movements, and more. It's a lot to think about, which is why you can't afford to "wing it" when showtime rolls around. Successful presentations depend on planning and practice, which is the purpose of rehearsing, which is the subject of the next chapter.

Chapter 11
Rehearsal

A kid carrying a violin case walks up to a policeman in New York City.

"Officer," the kid says, "how do I get to Carnegie Hall?"

The cop replies, "Practice, practice, practice."

Why Rehearse?

Musicians, actors, and dancers rehearse for countless hours both alone and with their ensembles. So do athletes and sports teams – they call it practice instead of rehearsal. For months before lift-off, space shuttle crews undergo a long course of rigorous training that includes meticulous rehearsals of each crucial operation of their mission. Armed forces rehearse endlessly, from training raw troops in basic combat operations to doing "dry runs" of planned operations. These and many other professions have a tradition of rehearsal … no questions asked … it's simply a given that the way to success is practice, practice, practice.

So it baffles me that so many business and professional presentations are given with little or no rehearsal. When I see someone make a speech that obviously wasn't rehearsed much, if at all, I ask myself, did he think the stakes were too low to justify the time it would take to practice, even just a little?

When are the stakes high enough to make it worth your while to rehearse?

Here's one answer: The stakes are high enough when there is an audience you care about and when you are taking up their precious time. Unrehearsed presentations, like the first draft of a piece of writing, tend to be long, flabby, repetitive, disjointed, and ultimately boring. Are you really willing to try the patience of your audience with such a performance? Why would you want to risk alienating them when your purpose is to persuade them?

Here's another answer: Every presentation you give in business and professional life shapes your reputation, your "personal brand." Are you okay with gaining a reputation for being tedious, confusing, or confused? Worse, are you willing to risk the joke that bombs, the quip that offends, the phrase that poisons the air for you, your company, your project, your purpose? Those are the mistakes that unrehearsed speakers make.

In addition to the granddaddy of all excuses – "There wasn't time" – I commonly hear a couple of other reasons why people don't rehearse. "I know this material backwards and forwards … I've given this presentation before … believe me, it just flows." But, I have to ask, is it well-organized and well-paced? Powerful and persuasive? Not too long and not too short for the allotted time? The last time you presented this material, did the audience give you the same high marks you gave yourself?

If you're good at thinking on your feet, you have an admirable skill. But I have an announcement: thinking-on-your-feet presentations are almost always inferior to those that are well and truly rehearsed. To invoke the analogy with writing one more time, how many first drafts have you written that didn't get better through revision and polishing?

I've also encountered people who sincerely believe that rehearsal makes them flat or fake or stale. "But what about my spontaneity?" they ask. I find that most of the people who use this argument have never rehearsed enough to actually experience a presentation's going flat and, if they did, it was probably because their rehearsal techniques were faulty. In any case, as audience members we've all experienced a lot more of the under-rehearsed than the over-rehearsed variety.

To be sure, with a heavily scripted presentation (especially one reviewed to within an inch of its life by the legal department), you start at a disadvantage. Others have chosen your words for you. You have not only to become familiar with those words but to "make them your own" so you can deliver them in a natural, relaxed, conversational style. Which means that this kind of presentation actually requires more rehearsal, not less.

Now that I've worn out my soapbox, I'll share what I believe is the number one, perfectly understandable, reason people don't rehearse business and professional presentations –

They don't know how.

That's what this chapter is about: efficient, effective techniques for preparing powerful, persuasive presentations through rehearsal.

Out Loud and on Your Feet

You can't rehearse in your head. Simply reading over your script or your notes isn't going to get you anywhere. You have to rehearse a speech out loud and, assuming that you're going to be delivering it standing up, that's how you need to rehearse it – on your feet. Even if you'll be presenting in a sit-down environment, like a panel discussion, you'll greatly energize yourself and your performance by rehearsing on your feet.

Ideally, you should rehearse under conditions as close as possible to those you'll be presenting in. You may not have access to an auditorium or a stage, but try at least to find a large space that will require you to project, vocally and physically. And of course, bring along an audience of at least one trusted colleague or friend, to give you objective feedback.

Approaching Rehearsal

Rehearsing is like going to the gym, the dance studio, or the driving range. It's a place to work on your strength, your skills, your game under conditions free of performance pressure. It's a time to try new ideas and techniques, take risks, make discoveries. In my experience, it can and should be great fun and enormously exciting, as over and over you find yourself making significant breakthroughs in both content and style while rehearsing.

When approaching rehearsal, keep in mind you can't rehearse everything at once, much less polish and improve everything. You can't test your objectives, reassess the obstacles, revamp the structure, tinker with your rhetoric, smooth out the flow, work on your vocal skills, and perfect your movements and gestures all at the same time.

Most people, I've found, tend to want to start the rehearsal process with a complete run-through of their presentation. I advise against this. Trying to slog through an entire presentation right out of the gate is exhausting and inefficient. In all likelihood, you won't even get through the first half before you run out of time or energy or both. Maybe that's why so many presentations start strong, then drift and finish weak.

Instead, I recommend rehearsing distinct elements of a presentation, one at a time, then assembling the elements into a complete, polished whole.

First and Most, Rehearse the Opening and the Close

As I emphasize in Chapter 8 and elsewhere, the opening and the close are the most important parts of any presentation. The opening is your chance – maybe your only chance – to seize command of the occasion and the attention of the audience. The close is what's most likely to be remembered, and your last chance to drive home your message and your call to action.

That alone is reason enough why you should rehearse your opening and your close first and most. But there's another reason, especially if you've structured your presentation as recommended in Chapter 8, using a hook, a promise, and a roadmap as your opening, and then closing with a recapitulation of the same elements. By rehearsing the opening and close, you effectively rehearse the body of your whole presentation. If you've incorporated your message mantra into both the opening and the close, you also get a chance to work on that important statement. If you've heightened your rhetoric for the opening and the close, which is a common and very effective tactic, you get a chance to hear how it sounds and dial it up or down to a level that's comfortable.

There's one more reason to rehearse your opening and close first and most: if that's all you have time to rehearse, you'll be prepared to give the whole presentation. You'll have maximized the benefit of your rehearsal time. In a pinch – if you have, say, only an hour or two to rehearse – always spend at least half your rehearsal time on your opening and your close.

Sharpen Your Hook and Close with a Bang

Here are my basic tips and techniques for rehearsing the two most important elements of any presentation – the things you should be sure you get right in your opening and close.

How often have you sat through an opening like this?

> Thank you ... um, George. Thanks for, uh, those kind words of introduction. Um – let's see ... just – get this – thing adjusted *[amplified sound of buffeting microphone]*. Okay. Now. What an event, huh? And what a place? What I want to do is, I want to start out by telling you a story – heh heh. It starts like this ...

In the theater, this is called *bleeding*. An actor can bleed *into* a moment or *out of* one (or both); either way, bleeding drains the life out of the drama, by exhausting the patience of the audience before the moment unfolds or undermining the moment's significance by letting it drift away. In the same way, bleeding can also deal a mortal blow to a presentation, especially at the opening.

My recommendation: Go right for the hook. Do not mention the occasion, the venue, or (heaven forbid) the weather. Do not even acknowledge the person who introduced you (if any) or the applause that greeted you (if any) except with a simple "Thank you." Then get on with it.

Let nothing get in the way. Go directly and immediately for the hook. And make it crisp. Some examples:

> "Thank you. *New York Times*, August 13th, 2004. Headline: 'HCA Executive Faces Criminal Probe. Indictment Expected.' The lead paragraph: 'The New York state attorney general will bring evidence this week to the grand jury ...'"

"Two months and five days ago, accompanied by an experienced wilderness guide, my father-in-law and I had just completed a glorious if arduous ascent up Mount Shasta – 14,162 feet above the floor of far Northern California. As we started to make our way down again, I took the lead – but after just a few minutes, I heard a strange sound from behind. I turned around to find that my father-in-law had disappeared."

"A transformation is upon us. It's everywhere. Even in something as simple [holding out his hand] as this wristwatch I'm wearing. Pretty much since I started wearing one, I've counted on my watch to give me the time. When the transformation I'm talking about is complete, I'll be able to count on it to give me a world of timely information."

It's just as important to finish strong as it is to open strong. And it's just as possible to let a close bleed off into boredom or insignificance. You don't want your audience to leave, physically or psychically, before you've finished.

I believe it's a good idea to give the audience a cue that you are "wrapping up;" by showing them a light at the end of the tunnel, you can actually sharpen their attention on your closing. But if you say things like "And finally" more than once or twice, or tell them pleadingly that you're "almost finished," your close will start to hemorrhage. The audience will start to feel that you're never going to finish, and they'll start to tune you out.

Oddly enough, the same thing will happen if you begin to hurry your close because you're running out of time. The audience will sense that you've given up on your close, if not your entire presentation, and they'll give up on it, too.

With a well-rehearsed close, you can treat your audience to something akin to the stirring last movement of a symphony. That's why it's important to rehearse your close early and often, so you can bring fresh energy and gusto to it, just as you will want to do in performance. Be sure to keep up the pace, but try varying the rhythm and cadence as well as your volume. Try adding a "pregnant pause" before a significant point or a transition. Discover and practice the gestures you can use to underline key words and phrases, animate your feelings, draw your audience to you. Try to end in one of your money positions.

Be sure to include the moment *after* you finish as part of your rehearsal, just as you should do in performance. Too often, presenters "cut and run" the instant they finish, as if they're relieved to be done or apologetic for taking the audience's time.

Instead, stand in there; the stage is still yours, so hold it a moment longer. By and large, an audience wants to show its appreciation for a job well done. So dare to wait for the applause. Sure, it doesn't always come, but when it does, accept it graciously. You and your audience will both feel more fulfilled.

Rehearse the Arc

The arc of your presentation is more than an outline (although it is that, too). The arc is your throughline, the driving train of information and logic that gives your presentation both momentum and coherence.

Rehearsing the arc enables you to see how all the sections of your presentation (and all the slides of your PowerPoint deck) fit together. At the same time, it puts you in touch with the importance and urgency of each of your objectives in turn. By helping you spot and expunge unnecessary tangents or forays into minutiae, rehearsing for arc also helps you tighten up your presentation.

Just as in other kinds of rehearsal, it's important to be on your feet and say the words out loud when rehearsing the arc. But when you rehearse the arc, you don't rehearse the *words* you'll use in your presentation. Instead, for every PowerPoint slide, note card, or key message, you simply state out loud what you intend to *achieve*.

Three examples of rehearsing the arc:

A presentation without slides

- I'll start by establishing the consumer's yearning for the connected entertainment experience.
- I'll define what connected entertainment means to me, personally.
- I'll use my personal story to suggest that a tipping point is at hand.
- Next, I'll establish the three things we'll achieve with our newest innovations—
    1. weave together content and devices,
    2. extend these experiences beyond personal enjoyment to enjoyment with a broader community, and
    3. vastly expand both the range of entertainment experiences and the community that enjoys them.
- I'll demonstrate the games, the live service, the expanding community, and the ability to reach out and capture movies, television, and music.
- Finally, I'll return to the tipping point theme and suggest that the launch of these innovations will accelerate our growth from a competitive option to a ubiquitous presence in digital entertainment.

A basic slide-by-slide presentation

Slide 1:   Deliver the hook, promise, and roadmap.

Slide 2:   Capture the imagination of the audience by describing the "nirvana experience."

Slide 3:   Show the current pain points.

Slide 4:   Establish our pedigree – we have the DNA to do this.

Slide 5:   The message here is that we have the right structure.

Slide 6:   Sell the leadership team – use stories.

Slide 7:   Define the investment we'll need to make.

Slide 8:   The key message here is that these investments have paid off before.

… and so forth.

A slide presentation with distinct sections

- Section 1: The first three slides establish the idea of the "burning platform." Here I'll use compelling data and one good story to create the sense of urgency.
  - This slide says our growth is slowing..
  - This slide shows our inefficiencies versus the market.
  - This slide shows the scary emergence of our competition.
- This is the pivot slide. It asks the question: What is to be done?
- Section 2: The next three slides are designed to give the audience hope that there are distinct actions we can take to turn the tide in our favor.
  - This slide proves that the market is still immense.
  - This slide shows the potential trajectory of our newest product.
  - This slide shows the impact my preferred efficiency initiative will have on productivity.
- Section 3: With the next three slides I'll go deeper into the staffing, resources, and timelines of our three initiatives.
  - This slide is a compelling description of the growth campaign.
  - This slide is deep dive into the alignment of incentives initiative.
  - This slide should convince folks we have a great product innovation roadmap.
- Section 4: The next two slides are all about actions.
  - This slide details the timelines, roles, and responsibilities for the rollout of our initiatives.
  - With this slide I call the audience to action.
- Close: The final slide paints a picture of our bright future once we've executed on our plan.

Although it may seem straightforward and even a bit dull, I cannot overemphasize the importance of rehearsing the arc. I've seen it work magic for countless clients. Spreading printouts of a slide show on a conference room table and using them to rehearse the arc seems to sear the objectives and flow of the presentation into your brain. And don't underestimate the power of having your arc down cold. When it comes time to make your presentation, it will help you keep up your pace, it will enable to get right back on track when people interrupt or ask questions, and it will make you far more compelling and persuasive.

Rehearse the Problem Sections

Once you've worked on your opening and close and gotten comfortable with the arc of your presentation, the next best use of your rehearsal time is to focus on those sections that need the most attention.

Chances are you'll know what your problem sections are, and your rehearsal audience can help you identify them as well. Your problem sections may be the most complex and therefore the most potentially confusing to your audience (if not to you). They may contain the most controversial or disruptive things you plan to say. They may be the new parts you've added to material you've presented before. They may not be "problem" sections so much as important sections that you want to be sure you have mastered.

Whatever the case, identify your problem sections and rehearse them, one at a time, until you're confident that you've got them down cold.

Physical Rehearsal

Good public speakers make their audiences comfortable by being comfortable themselves – comfortable in their own skins, that is, physically comfortable in their bodies and in the space they occupy. That's why physical rehearsal is important.

Physical rehearsal is your chance to decide, What are you going to do with your body during your presentation? Sit or stand? Where? How? Move from one place to another? When? How? If you're using PowerPoint, how can you make sure the audience pays attention to you as well as the slides without getting in the way? Are there moments you want to emphasize with a particular gesture? Are you sure that gesture works for that moment? How big should the gesture be? Physical rehearsal is your chance to try out various movements and gestures, figure out which ones work best, and practice them so that they feel natural.

Start by practicing your entrance. If that sounds silly, remember that you are an actor, a performer in your own show, and first impressions are crucial. How you enter from "nowhere" to "here," being the first thing your audience observes, will be the first thing that shapes their perception of you and your presentation.

Next, rehearse the opening and close of your presentation, but this time focus on your staging – where you stand, when and where you move, your body language and gestures. Remember your "money" positions – three distinct places in the performance space where you look powerful (and where you can be seen and heard by everyone, of course), discussed in Chapter 10 – and put them to use during your all-important opening and close.

Rehearse the arc of your presentation with your focus on the staging. Decide what sections you'll present from each of your money positions, and figure out when and how you'll move from one to another. The idea is to add variety to what the audience is watching – you. Nothing commands an audience's attention like movement, but as I emphasize in Chapter 10, you don't want to wander aimlessly. Your movements must have "definition" – start, go, stop. That doesn't mean you have to rush, and it doesn't mean you should stop talking as you move. Indeed, a speaker "on a stroll," who can walk and talk and maintain rapport with an audience all at the same time, is a speaker that audiences cannot ignore.

Spend some time working on your gestures. Here again, you'll need the help and feedback of your rehearsal audience. Are there parts of your presentation that would benefit from more animation? What kind of gestures work best for you and best for your most important moments? Try out various gestures to see how they work for you and your audience.

Meanwhile, root out your physical tics. Are you fidgeting with your pen, staring off into space when you pause for breath, swaying when you stand? Urge your rehearsal audience to be ruthless in pointing out such faults.

Finally, be sure to practice with the tools and technologies you'll be using, if any: microphone and microphone stand, remote control, laser pointer, overhead projector, flip chart, mouse, controller, whatever.

Vocal Rehearsal

By rehearsing your presentation verbatim as much as possible, you do more than "get used to" saying the words (although that is no small thing). You also get to experiment, to take risks, to make mistakes and make discoveries.

Review Chapter 9, "The Power of Voice." In vocal rehearsal, you want to work on your projection and articulation. Ask your rehearsal audience to sit in the back row. Can they hear and understand every word from back there? Don't forget to ask for their help in eliminating verbal tics like "um" or "uh," "okay" or "well." Make sure they bust you for saying "kinda" and "sorta," for starting sentences with "Basically," and for overusing empty, overused adjectives like "amazing" and "incredible."

Work on varying your volume, pitch, pace, and cadence to support the content of your presentation. Don't hold back; it's by trying out bold vocal choices that you'll often discover your best stuff. There's an old theater tradition called the Italian run-through, in which the actors zip through the dialogue at double or triple normal speed, often indulging in big, over-the-top gestures and emotions at the same time. I recommend that you make this exercise part of your vocal rehearsal, especially if you have a tendency to be too deliberate or to speak in a steady, even tone, which audiences find boring.

Aside from being lots of fun for you and your rehearsal audience, doing an Italian run-through will unleash reserves of energy you didn't know you have. You'll probably be surprised at just how many over-the-top elements your audience tells you to "keep in." You may find yourself taking your presentation to an entirely new level.

After Rehearsal, Before Showtime

Don't confuse rehearsal with performance.

Rehearsal tends to be a technical process, requiring you to focus on specific elements of your presentation and performance – the open and close, structure, posture, movement, voice, gesture, and all the rest. You'll probably find yourself watching yourself during rehearsals. In the theater, we call this the "third eye." A helpful if not essential tool, it's the awareness of how you look and sound that enables you to shape and improve your presentation. But it's dangerous, too, because it can seduce you into a kind of self-consciousness that can undermine your performance.

As you move from rehearsal to performance, shrink the third eye. Put your concerns about technique out of your mind, and have faith that the practice you've put in will "be there" for you at showtime.

During performance, your primary concern must be "Are they getting the message?" Not "How am I doing?" or "Do they like me?" Remember, the most important person in the room is not you ... it's your audience. Focus on them, and talk with them. Keep it simple. Stay with your objectives. Hold your message mantra close. And let all the "technical" stuff take care of itself.

To get to Carnegie Hall, every kid with a violin has to practice, practice, practice. Once she arrives on that great stage, however, her job is not to share the secrets of her technique but simply to play the music. Like great musicians, great presenters forget all about rehearsal when it's showtime. They know that all the preparation they've done will stand them in good stead. They simply perform.

Chapter 12
Winning Q&A Techniques

Many presentations include a question-and-answer session. Whenever this is the case, *it is essential that you view the Q&A as part of your presentation*. There's nothing worse than giving a great speech only to have everything go south during the Q&A because you flub a question you're not ready for, stray from or get pushed off your message, or lose control of the whole occasion in the face of hostile or aggressive questioning. You must prepare for the Q&A every bit as hard as you do for the body of your presentation.

The point is not to try to anticipate every possible question or arm yourself to fend off the barbarians. Think positively about the Q&A; after all, it's a wonderful opportunity to drive your message home.

Every Question Is an Opportunity

When helping them prepare for Q&A, I like to start by reminding my clients that for every question there are many, many answers. How you answer a question is your choice. In fact, you also have the right not to answer any question you don't want to answer.

In any case, it's not your responsibility to answer questions the way we all did as schoolchildren – that is, in order to please the questioner. Instead, your mission is to use every question as an occasion for saying what you want to say. As you approach Q&A, turn the tables on the audience by keeping in mind this question for *them*: "What questions do you have for my answers?" And during Q&A, keep this option handy and use it whenever you want: don't answer the question they asked; answer the question they should have asked.

You'll find that you can answer many if not most questions by repeating something you've already said in your presentation – taking the opportunity to repeat a key message. When a question requires you to give more information about a topic that you've already addressed, go ahead – but be careful not to over-elaborate or wander off on a tangent. Instead, transition quickly from the "new" information to the message it clarifies or supports. Keep your message mantra front and center in your awareness during Q&A, and reinforce it at every opportunity.

And what if no one is ready to ask a question or if you don't get the questions you want? Make sure you have *your own* questions at the ready, such as –

"You may be wondering …"

                or

"One question that I've spent some time thinking about is …"

Again, Q&A is an opportunity for you to reinforce *your* messages. If the audience is slow to take you up on it, ask and answer the questions *you* want to address. Chances are, that will prime the pump and the audience will soon join in the dialogue.

A Q&A Playbook

There are many techniques for handling Q&A not just successfully but gracefully. Starting with some baseline tips and then proceeding to ways of handling specific types of questions and situations, here's my playbook for Q&A.

Body language. Keep an open posture; don't hide your hands or cross your arms.

Tone and attitude. You need the same tone and attitude during Q&A as during a presentation: confident, passionate, informative, interactive. Q&A is a time for you to shine; take advantage of it. Remember, you are the expert.

You are also the audience's friend; Q&A is a great time to come out from behind the podium or table, move toward your audience, engage them more personally as a group and as individuals. Use people's names if you know them. Start each answer by responding directly to the questioner, but as you transition to a more general point (ideally, one of your key messages from the body of the presentation), take in the whole audience.

Active listening. Remember that your listening will be judged as much as your answers. Listen to *the questioner*, not just the question, with an open body posture, good eye contact, and a display of genuine interest.

Listen carefully. Take time to hear the question and make sure you understand it before responding. Ask the questioner to clarify if necessary. A tried-and-true technique for starting an answer is to repeat the question. In larger venues where the audience may not be able to hear every question from the floor, you may have to repeat the question so that everyone will understand your answer.

"Gosh, I like you!" While you're listening to and answering questions, think about how much you like the audience or the person asking the questions. Thinking "Gosh, I like you!" will give you sparkle and may even inspire you to smile. This simple technique is especially useful in on-camera interviews, because what you're thinking and feeling is easy to read in your face close-up. It will also give you the extra energy you need in the two-dimensional realm of video.

Start with the conclusion. During Q&A, people don't have the time or the patience to wait for you to build to a conclusion.

Say it and stop. Especially during hostile or potentially hostile Q&A, always give your best answer and *stop*. Professional interviewers – including lawyers taking depositions, news reporters, and financial analysts – are practiced in using silence to intimidate and draw people into saying more than they need or want to. Don't give in.

Define, don't defend. Questioners sometimes want to focus on the "negatives" – past mistakes or failures, opportunities missed, uncertainties, and so forth. Don't be defensive, and don't be drawn into dissecting the past. When you start talking about why something's broken, it's all too easy to start assigning blame. Instead, focus what has been learned or what you're doing to overcome the challenges or do better. Define the promise of the future rather than defending against the disappointments of the past.

Buy time. You can't anticipate every question; audience members come up with the darndest things. There will be times when you're surprised or caught off guard by a question or comment from the audience. Don't panic or hurry your answer – you may live to regret it. Instead, buy time to think about your answer. There are three ways to buy time:

- Ask the person to repeat the question.
- Rephrase the question in a way you wish to answer it. Again, don't answer the question they asked; answer the question they should have asked.
- Take time to consider your answer before speaking.

Though least used, the third technique is actually the most powerful. Taking your time, being deliberate, gives you an air of authority. It also adds to your credibility, because the audience sees that you're actually thinking about the question and not just spewing out some prepackaged pabulum.

Touch and go. Touch on the question you've been asked and then bridge to the message you want to deliver. (For a look at some masters of this technique, just tune into a press briefing on C-SPAN or a Sunday morning talk show.) Here are some reliable bridging phrases for transitioning to your message:

- "The real story here is …"
- "But there's a bigger issue here …"
- "What you might not know is …"
- "As I said during my presentation, we're more interested in …"
- "But I'd like to get back to what's really important …"

If you don't know the answer, say so. Never try to answer a question when you don't know the answer. During friendly Q&A it's perfectly okay to say, "Good question – I really don't have an answer. But …" – and then you can promise the questioner to find the answer later, and/or transition the dialogue to a topic that is "solid ground" for you.

Questions You Don't Have to Answer

People sometimes ask inappropriate questions – questions that you won't want to answer for any number of reasons. They may try to blindside you with new information or a "phantom authority" – for example, "According to the recent article in …" Or they may ask questions in such a way as to trick you, trap you, or box you in – for example, "Is that true or not?"

Always remember that you don't have to answer *any* question you don't want to answer. At the same time, there are graceful ways to avoid answering troublesome, "trick," or "trap" questions while turning them into opportunities.

In general, all you have to do is transition from your refusal (with or without giving your reason) to something you do want to talk about. Here are several examples:

Q: Seeks proprietary information.
A: "That's proprietary information that I can't share with you, but what I can tell you is …"

Q: Asks for a legal opinion or information.
A: "That's a legal issue and I'm not a lawyer. But I can say …"

Q: Probes for information about a specific employee.
A: "We don't speak publicly about personnel issues. What I can tell you is …"

Q: Probes for information about a particular individual.
A: "Out of respect for Mr. Smith's privacy, I'm afraid I can't address that.

Perhaps he'd be willing to discuss it with you. In the meantime, what I want to emphasize is …"

Q: "What if…?"
A: "I wouldn't want to speculate."

Q: "When will you stop strong-arming Alpha Corporation …?"
A: "We have a very good relationship with Alpha Corporation, and …"
or "We think competition is good for both our industry and our customers …"

Q: "What three mistakes…?
A: "What we should be talking about are our three greatest successes …"

Q: "How would X respond?"
A: "You'll have to ask X."

Q: "What is the worst…?"
A: "That would be speculating. Let's focus on the real issue here …"

Q: "It was recently stated that …" or "An article in the *News* last week said …"
A: "I haven't heard that …" or "I haven't seen that article."

Q: "… yes or no?" or "Is that true?"
A: "In fact, that's not a yes or no question…" or "I don't think it's as simple as that. When we look at all the facts …"

How to Handle Hostile Questioners and Tough Questions

Not all Q & A is friendly. You never know where or when a "crankster" or "pot-stirrer" will appear. Always anticipate hostile questions, no matter what the topic or the venue.

When you sense hostility in a question or questioner, first remind yourself to maintain your key communication techniques: an open and relaxed posture, a resonant and varied voice, concise and clear answers.

Consider your options. Again, you don't have to answer any question, especially one that's off-topic or clearly intended to "set you up" to make a mistake, put you on the defensive, or lead to another hostile question.

Of course, not all challenging questions come from people who are "out to get you." In business and professional life, just as everywhere else, bad things happen, mistakes get made, people are disappointed or hurt. If you're conducting a Q&A in the wake of such difficulties, you may have to deal with the tough questions that result. In these circumstance, questioners often express anger or frustration. The best way to deal with such moments is an approach I call *empathy without culpability.*

First, you acknowledge the feeling that's being expressed: "I see this is really upsetting to you." Then you empathize: "I am deeply saddened by your experience … " or " I think everyone here can relate to your frustration." Finally, you bridge from the negative to the positive, which often means from the past to the future: "Our big concern now is moving forward and building a better …"

Through empathy without culpability, you validate the feelings of those asking tough questions *without* agreeing to take the blame. Sometimes, however, questioners will raise the ante on you. Their feelings of disappointment, hurt, or frustration will escalate to the level of accusation. You'll start to feel that the boundary between you and the problem is disappearing, and you may be tempted to cut short the discussion by saying something like "Let's take that offline." I recommend, instead, a technique known as *triangulation.*

Triangulation is a matter of separating yourself from the problem. This can be done most easily by writing out the problem or issue on a white board or flip chart. If that's not possible, you must use language that clearly and deliberately places the problem somewhere other than within you. Once you've separated yourself from the problem, you then turn and face the problem side by side with your questioner – literally or figuratively. "Now, I think I've put the question up on the board as you described it. Let's take a look together and see how we can solve it." Through triangulation, you change the nature of the engagement from "you against me" to "us versus it."

In any case, never allow Q&A to become a dialogue between you and just one questioner. Don't let a questioner with an agenda follow up with a second question. Instead, take control by transitioning to another section of the audience: "So as you can see, we're working hard to tackle that challenge … (turning your body away from the questioner) "… now I think I saw that you had a question over here. How can I help you?"

When Being Interviewed by the Media

As a media trainer, I recommend that you avoid the always perilous and rarely fair-minded world of the media without first going through rigorous preparation and coaching.

That said, we live in a world of video cell phones, blogs and YouTube, where the media, professional and non-, may take you unawares. So a few survival techniques are in order –

Control the Q&A. Use the principles I've already mentioned: "What questions do you have for my answers?" Don't answer the question they asked; answer the question they should have asked.

Understand the new ground rules. Dealing with professional (and non-professional) journalists is a form of Q&A with its own special challenges. It is not a conversation. That means you cannot build on ideas. They can't print what you don't say; but by the same token, you can't count on their printing *everything* you do say. When they appear in the media, your statements may not be placed in the context of any previous or following statements you made. As a rule of thumb, try to make sure that anything you say would be complete and make sense if printed on a billboard by the freeway (your message mantra can come in handy here). In other words, you have to be your own editor – and a rigorous one at that.

Correct false assumptions/statements. When an interviewer states a false assumption, stop him or her and establish the real facts before going on.

Don't repeat poison words. If any interviewer uses a term like "failure" or "train wreck," your job is to come back with language that changes the tone – for example, "opportunity" or "setback."

Don't break into jail. Avoid bringing up new issues or perspectives that might draw the interviewer away from your message. Above all, stay away from topics that are too complicated or potentially controversial, or introduce a competitor's point of view.

No jargon or acronyms. Your business or profession, like most these days, is probably rife with jargon, acronyms, and assorted insider language. If you want to be quoted in the press, speak in plain language that the general reader will understand.

Never get drawn into a fight. As Mark Twain is reputed to have said, "Never pick a fight with someone who buys ink by the barrel." Argue with a reporter or interviewer and you will lose – it's as simple as that.

No sarcasm. More than one career has been ruined by a snide remark or poisonous quip that took on a life of its own in media.

Be careful about jokes. Humor doesn't always "play" in print or even on video. Besides, humor can be double-edged. What's funny to you may be confusing or even insulting to someone else. Before using humor in front of the press (or any audience, for that matter), pre-test it with a trusted colleague.

Never lie. Reporters don't like to be lied to any more than anyone else — except perhaps the ones who know they can make their reputation by catching you out in a lie.

Finale
It's Showtime!

There's no business like show business
Like no business I know
Everything about it is appealing
Everything the traffic will allow
Nowhere can you have that happy feeling
When you aren't stealing that extra bow …
– from Irving Berlin's "Annie Get Your Gun"

If an actor ever tells you he doesn't get excited on opening night, either he's lying or he's missing out on one of the greatest thrills of his vocation.

As a presenter, you too will have your opening nights – with your talent, your goals, your reputation on the line … and any number of critics ready to judge you, whether in the hallways and offices or in print, online, and on the street.

As the clock ticks down and the audience settles in, your heart beats faster – just as it should. After all, if you don't care enough to be nervous and excited, you're probably not very invested in your presentation or your objective, and your chances of success are slim.

But how should you handle the excitement, the nerves, the sheer energy of those trying moments?

In the theater you would be guided by the director, who usually shares some final words with the cast, such as –

"Remember, the most important people in the room are not you, but the audience."

"You've done all you can – now just tell the story."

"And remember, whatever else you do out there, have fun!"

In sports the coach usually takes the lead, sending his players out of the locker room with inspiring slogans such as –

"This is the moment when all your hard work pays off."

"Have faith in yourself and your team."

"Hearts on fire, brains on ice!"

But when making a presentation, you're usually very much alone in those hours and moments that lead up to showtime. What should you say to yourself? What should you do with all that nervous energy?

You may be tempted to go over various parts of your presentation or review your technique. You might find yourself checking your notes, thinking about your opening sentence, going over a pivotal story, or trying out different ways of saying your message mantra. The impulse to check and recheck the details is natural. After all, aren't those the lines of your parachute, the only thing that will keep you from crashing and burning? Shouldn't you check your gear one more time to make sure that it's all in order, all buttoned up, all secure?

No.

You are prepared. You have done everything you can to guarantee success. You're in touch with your professional passion, ready to bring it to the stage and share it with your audience. You know what you want to achieve and that you're ready to achieve it. You've played detective, listened to others, done your home-work. You know your audience – who they are, what they expect, what they need and want. You've identified the obstacles to success and you're fully equipped to overcome them.

You know what you want to say. You've taken a fire hose of information and reduced and refined it, crafting a message that is crisp, compelling, and memorable – and now you're about to present that message, like a gift, to your audience. You've taken care that your presentation is expertly structured, easy for you to navigate and easy for the audience to follow, understand, and remember.

You are confident. Through rehearsal, you've gone from worrying about what to say to perfecting how to say it. You've made good choices about staging and gestures, your pacing, your tone, and you've made sure all those choices work. Now you're poised to deliver a presentation that is engaging, artful, and persuasive. And you're secure in your readiness to handle any questions that may come during or after it.

There are two reasons to avoid fussing about details just before you "go on." First, by doing so you focus on the past – at the very moment when you need to be *completely in the present*. Second, details are really about technique, not perfor-mance. Music, theater, and dance audiences are not interested in a performer's technique; indeed, audiences can easily spot a performer who's showing off his or her technical prowess, and it almost always puts them off instead of drawing them in. The audience is there for the *performance,* not the performer; they want to see your character, not you ... to hear the story, not you telling it ... to give themselves up to the music, not the musicianship. The same is true in business and professional presentations. Audiences have little tolerance for presenters who are fixated on technique, who are clearly more worried about themselves than about the audience. An audience wants you to speak to them, move them, provoke them, persuade them.

At the beginning of many of my workshops, I play a simple game with the group. We toss an *imaginary* ball from person to person, each one saying the name of the person he or she is tossing the ball to. As the game progresses, we add another ball, then another, and another ... As the group learns to track several balls flying every which way, a lesson emerges: *To be successful you have to connect.* To pass a ball safely from your hands to another's, you *both* have to communicate through the entire act of tossing and catching. Which means that, as an individual, you cannot succeed by playing catch at the others in the group; you can succeed only by playing catch *with* them.

As the curtain rises, there is only one thing you need to do to succeed. Commit to connecting with your audience – *right here, right now, in the moment.* Dare to be present, to play catch with them, to have faith in all the hard work you've done to get to this moment – and then who needs a parachute?

Take a deep breath ... trust in your passion and your preparation ... let your energy flow from you to your audience ... stretch your wings ... and fly!

It's showtime!

Appendix 1
Top 10 Ways to Handle Nerves

1. Practice and rehearse your material – more than you think you need to. This includes talking through and visualizing the arc of your presentation (see Chapter 11).
2. Arrive early to set up the room and test the equipment.
3. Having arrived early, greet the audience as they arrive. Engage, chat, and make connections. When you begin speaking, use those people you've talked to as your "safe harbors" in the audience – friendly faces you can focus on for reassurance.
4. Be clear about and focus on your objectives – what do you want from the audience? Remember, it's about them, not you.
5. Breathe. (A good physical warm up, workout, or long walk the morning before a high-stakes presentation will help prepare and relax you.) Take a deep breath right before you begin.
6. Remember your "money positions" (see Chapter 9) and get into one before starting to speak.
7. Start with a story. Stories are easy to tell and give you access to your best, most relaxed communication style.
8. Within the first two minutes, shift the focus from you to the audience. If appropriate, ask them to discuss something at their tables.
9. Go ahead and admit to your own nervousness – if the situation is appropriate.
10. Carry your notes and give yourself permission to refer to them as often as you want or need to.

Bonus tip: When yours is one of several presentations on the program, requiring you to sit and wait before you go on, actively listen to and engage in the presentations prior to yours by taking notes rather than ruminating on your own material or performance. This will help keep you in the present and prevent you from working yourself into a tizzy.

Appendix 2
Presentation Effectiveness Worksheet

This worksheet covers the key characteristics of an effective presentation.

Ask your friends and colleagues to use it to provide feedback about your presentations during rehearsal and/or performance. You may also wish to use it yourself to make notes about speeches and presentations that you attend as an audience member, as a way of developing your eye and ear for what makes a presentation effective and persuasive.

Speaker: _____

Presentation title or topic:

_____

Date: _____

Compelling

Does the speaker capture and command the attention of the audience? How?

Strong Objective

Does the speaker seem to have a clear objective? What is it?

On Task

Does the speaker stay on course and repeat the key messages?

Use of Physical Space

Does the speaker use the space performance space effectively, moving and positioning himself or herself to provide variety and enhance meaning?

Use of Visuals

How does the speaker use visuals to enhance the presentation? Are they effective? Does the speaker interact with the visuals in an effective manner?

Gestures

Does the speaker use physical life and gestures effectively to enhance delivery? How?

Connection

Does the speaker connect with the audience, through good eye contact and/or by other means?

Relaxation

Does the speaker seem relaxed?

Language

How does the speaker use language clearly and forcefully? What
phrases or choices of words are most effective? What choices,
such as excessive jargon or unexplained acronyms, create confusion
or otherwise detract from the presentation?

Voice

Does the speaker project his or her voice well, and in a pleasing
tone?
Does the speaker use any of the following vocal techniques effectively?
- Volume variations
- Pitch variations
- Inflection variations
- Rate/cadence variations, including dramatic pauses

Owning the Talk

Does the speaker personalize the presentation and make it his or
her own, or does it seem like a "canned" talk?

The Whole Package

Is the speaker's combined physical, vocal, and intellectual energy
sufficient to engage and move the audience?

Appendix 3
Techniques for Handling Challenging Situations

Chapter 12, "Winning Q&A Techniques," provides several tips on dealing with challenging, disruptive, or downright hostile post-presentation questions from audience members, journalists, and others. The techniques described here are more tailored to interactive, workshop-style presentations and training sessions, where your audience plays a more collaborative role – and where their resistance or reluctance to cooperate can undermine your authority and torpedo your goals.

PASSIVE RESISTANCE		
What you see or hear	**What to do**	**What to say**
• Doing other work (PDA, Blackberry, etc.)	• Be compelling from the moment you begin.	• *Can I have your undivided attention up front please?*
• Answering pages	• Stand in front of or next to the unengaged person.	• *Let's begin so we can end on time.*
	• Use the person as an example (call him/her by name).	• *Let's begin the exercise... now! Or* (holding a stop watch) *Ready... set... go!*
• Slow to engage in the exercises		
	• Engage a familiar or supportive participant.	• *I know that people like Bob are in that situation all the time. How does it work for you, Bob?*
• Silent when asked to respond		• *Is everyone clear on what I said?*
• Blank looks when asked a question	• Use body language or eye contact to send a message.	• *You look confused. How can I help?*

PASSIVE-AGGRESSIVE RESISTANCE

What you see or hear	What to do	What to say
Types of questions: • **Speculative**: "Why haven't we spent more on ...?" • **Hypothetical**: "So if I make those calls, what time do you think I'll get home to my family?" • **Vague**: "Where is this supposed to fit in the overall strategy for this organization?" • **Non-questions or statements:** "This means much more work ..." **Disruptive conversations or debate**: • "Those examples aren't realistic." • "Here's how I do it ..." • "This means much more work!" • "I'm already at my max, how do you expect me to ...?" • "This is pretty basic ..." • "We already did this program ..." • "I don't understand ... **Externalizing ("The Blame Game")** • "It's the others who need this training."	• *A multi-pronged approach to the passive-aggressive:* • **Accept** the offer. • **Buy time** if necessary. • **Engage** the issue using your experience/expertise and, if successful, engage the group. • **Engage** the group to flesh out and grapple with the situation. • **Bridge back** to your teaching objective. • Use your best judgment to determine how beneficial it will be to engage and flesh out the situation. Engage only if you believe you can do so without losing your forward momentum. • When engaging a problem, put the problem up on the board, thereby separating yourself from the problem. This creates a triangle and an opportunity for you and the participants to solve the problem *together*.	***Accept*** • *Thank you.* • *I'm hearing you say ...* • *That's a great point!* ***Buy time*** • *Let me see if I heard you correctly ...* • *I'm not sure I understand – will you repeat the question?* • *I think the real question is ...* • *Let me think about that for a second ...* ***Engage solo*** • *Actually...* • *That's one point of view, I believe.* • *In my experience, I've ...* • *That's exactly how I looked at it until ...* • *The way I've handled that situation is...* • *I've found it helpful to ...* ***Engage the group*** • *Do others share this experience?* • *How many of you have the same experience/concern?* • *How have you handled this situation before?* • *Let's brainstorm about this.*

• "Doing this isn't going to make up for the fact that we've got a bigger problem." • "If 'they' would just get their act together …"		***Bridging back to your objective*** • *Getting back to…* • *Let's talk about what we can do …* • *In the interest of time, I'm going to wrap this conversation up and move on to …* • *[Topic] is what we're here for today, so let's …*

AGGRESSIVE RESISTANCE

What you see or hear	What to do	What to say
Types of questions: • **Loaded:** "We all learned this in our training. Why are we talking about the basics?" • **Locked-in-a-box**: "Is this remedial punishment or some way of making us all do more work?" • **Leading**: "Do you have any idea who you're talking to?" • **Multiple**: "Do we have data to prove that? Has anyone linked that to …? Is this the best way to spend our resources? Have we thought about alternative ways of …? *Other blatantly antagonistic behavior:* • Refusing to participate • Taking a non-work-related phone call • Rabble-rousing.	• Stay calm. • Call out blatantly aggressive behavior. • Determine if it's really up to you to answer the questions. If not, "punt." • Consider your options: You may choose to engage or you may ignore. • Get out of the box. • Correct false assumptions and bridge to your objective. • Ignore or reframe. • Break down multiple questions and answer one at a time or "park" one or more questions for later consideration. • Engage directly with behavior, engage and ask for behavior change, or exit.	• *It sounds like you have some real concerns.* • *It seems you're upset about some aspect of this program. Let's talk about it afterwards because I want to hear your perspective.* • *This is a workshop about [topic]. (Perhaps go on to add –) If you don't wish to continue, feel free to leave.* • *I'm certain each department has its unique challenges; the real question is, what can all of us do to …* • *Wow – that's a whole bunch of questions, Jane. Let's take them one at a time.*

		• *Obviously, you have quite a few questions that need addressing. We're going to have to talk at the break and I'll try to address them one by one.*
		• *Paul, we can't continue while you're on your cell phone…*
		• *If you're unwilling to participate in the exercise, you're welcome to leave now.*
		• *Chris, I'm doing my best to teach this workshop and your behavior is interfering. Will you please stop?*

About the Author

Richard Butterfield (www.butterfieldspeaks.com) enjoys growing influence as a high-stakes communications coach to corporate leaders, lawyers, and other professionals. Following a successful stage career, for over a decade he has conducted countless workshops and coaching sessions for business executives, doctors, lawyers, entrepreneurs, and others. His client list includes Microsoft vice presidents and CEOs of companies such as Kaiser Permanente, Gartner Inc., Tenet Healthcare, Clif Bar Inc., CNET, The Cleveland Clinic, and Infospace, plus leaders at Genentech, Bayer Corporation, VISA, and Charles Schwab, and law firms Fenwick & West LLP, Sidley Austin LLP, and Liebert Cassidy Whitmore LLP.

Richard works with individuals and teams as they develop and prepare for product launches, funding pitches, financial presentations, thought leadership speeches, IPO roadshows, and book tours, and prepares lawyers and witnesses for the courtroom.

Richard's approach to persuasive presentations draws on his extensive experience as an actor, acting teacher, and director and is informed by a decade of public relations and marketing experience. A Stanford University graduate, he received his master's degree from the renowned American Conservatory Theater MFA program, where he later served as Conservatory Dean.

Richard Butterfield lives in a historic Victorian farmhouse in San Francisco's Bernal Heights neighborhood along with his wife Glynn, a film and video producer, daughter Judy, a highly regarded cabaret performer, and son Duke, a budding actor and player of classical guitar.

About the Editor

With more than 25 years as a professional writer, project manager, and communications consultant, Steven Young has created marketing and corporate communications for a wide range of businesses, from start-ups to the Fortune 500.

Steve has written advertising, direct response, and email campaigns, developed and executed branding and positioning strategies, and written and produced commercial radio spots, corporate and sales videos, and websites. As an executive speechwriter, he has written keynote addresses, stump speeches, analyst presentations, press briefings, and commencement addresses. His client list includes scores of consumer and technology companies, from big names like Apple, Electronic Arts, Microsoft, and SanDisk to nascent ventures such as Fonality and Jajah, as well as IT publishing and research organizations, venture firms, and non-profit institutions including Stanford University, the Graduate Theological Union, and the Rockefeller Foundation.

Steve maintains a website at www.stevenyoung.com.

Acknowledgements

While I do not consider myself a great writer, I can usually make my point on paper with clarity and even a certain panache. Contrary to her belief, perhaps, it appears that I really did learn something in Mrs. Bissell's 6th grade classroom at the Derby Academy. I suppose I picked up a pointer or two in high school English as well; I really can't recall. One experience I do remember is my freshman English section at Stanford, "Theater Inside Out" – a nifty title and a remarkable class taught by Steven Young.

Dramatic, witty, occasionally biting in his criticism, Steve hammered home the basics and inspired the poetic. That was in 1977. Fast-forward 20 years or more, and we found ourselves working together to help business leaders tell their stories, lead their organizations, influence their industries – Steve as a speechwriter and I as a communications consultant and presentation coach. Thus there was both logic and symmetry in my turning to Steve to edit *It's Showtime!*

Artful, expansive, and insightful in his suggestions and criticism, Steve has made a significant contribution to this book. Thanks, Steve.

It's Showtime! represents the passing on to me of timeless wisdom and proven techniques by my many mentors in the craft of acting and the art of the theater, including William Ball, Edward Hastings, Larry Hecht, Deborah Sussell, Albert Takazauckas, and John C. Fletcher.

The deepest insights come from experience, and I have all my clients to thank for inviting me into their own worlds of high-stakes communications. They include but are not limited to the folks at Liebert Cassidy, Microsoft, Clif Bar, Genentech, Gartner, Fenwick & West, Infospace, and Charles Schwab and the many people I've worked with and learned from in the world of public relations.

This book would never have come to be if not for the investment of time and energy of several leaders at Kaiser Permanente, who pushed me to put on paper what was a series of spoken-word workshops. Helen Crothers and Dr. Rae Oser have contributed mightily to both the content and clarity of *It's Showtime!*.

And loving thanks to my entire family.